# Empowering Teacher Leadership

This book explores how school leaders—both formal and informal—can create a supportive culture that leverages teamwork and empowers teachers to become leaders. By focusing on three foundational principles—empowerment, collegiality, and risk taking—schools can develop and enhance educators' capacity for success. With this practical resource, you will learn intentional and actionable strategies that empower participation in leadership at all levels through peer observation and team action planning. The book's chapters explore how to create systems that support trusting relationships, inspire distributed leadership, provide a vehicle for teachers to learn from each other and take risks, and develop informal and formal teacher leaders. This book provides a positive and proactive approach to collaborative school leadership that will invigorate your school community to work together more effectively for improved student outcomes. Rich reflection questions in each chapter help readers conceptualize the information presented and take actionable steps toward improvement.

Additional tools are available online for easy download here: www.routledge.com/9781032040554.

**Jeremy D. Visone** is Assistant Professor of Educational Leadership, Policy & Instructional Technology; Partnership Liaison; and Coordinator of the Internship in Educational Leadership at Central Connecticut State University, New Britain, CT, USA. He is a former principal of a National Blue Ribbon School.

# Other Eye On Education Books Available from Routledge
(www.routledge.com/eyeoneducation)

**The Confident School Leader**
Kara Knight

**Get Organized Digitally! The Educator's Guide to Time Management**
Frank Buck

**Creating, Grading, and Using Virtual Assessments:
Strategies for Success in the K-12 Classroom**
Kate Wolfe Maxlow, Karen L. Sanzo, and James Maxlow

**Leadership for Deeper Learning: Facilitating
School Innovation and Transformation**
Jayson Richardson, Justin Bathon, and Scott McLeod

**A Practical Guide to Leading Green Schools: Partnering with
Nature to Create Vibrant, Flourishing, Sustainable Schools**
Cynthia L. Uline and Lisa A. W. Kensler

**Building Learning Capacity in an Age of Uncertainty:
Leading an Agile and Adaptive School**
James A. Bailey

**Rural America's Pathways to College and Career: Steps
for Student Success and School Improvement**
Rick Dalton

**Bringing Innovative Practices to Your School: Lessons from International Schools**
Jayson W. Richardson

**A Guide to Impactful Teacher Evaluations: Let's Finally Get It Right!**
Joseph O. Rodgers

**A Guide to Early College and Dual Enrollment Programs: Designing
and Implementing Programs for Student Achievement**
Russ Olwell

**A Leadership Guide to Navigating the Unknown in
Education: New Narratives Amid COVID-19**
Sally J. Zepeda and Phillip D. Lanoue

**Leadership for Remote Learning**
Ronald Williamson and Barbara R. Blackburn

**The Strategy Playbook for Educational Leaders: Principles and Processes**
Isobel Stevenson and Jennie Weiner

# Empowering Teacher Leadership

Strategies and Systems to Realize
Your School's Potential

Jeremy D. Visone

NEW YORK AND LONDON

First published 2022
by Routledge
605 Third Avenue, New York, NY 10158

and by Routledge
2 Park Square, Milton Park, Abingdon, Oxon, OX14 4RN

*Routledge is an imprint of the Taylor & Francis Group, an informa business*

© 2022 Jeremy D. Visone

The right of Jeremy D. Visone to be identified as author of this work has been asserted in accordance with sections 77 and 78 of the Copyright, Designs and Patents Act 1988.

All rights reserved. No part of this book may be reprinted or reproduced or utilised in any form or by any electronic, mechanical, or other means, now known or hereafter invented, including photocopying and recording, or in any information storage or retrieval system, without permission in writing from the publishers.

*Trademark notice*: Product or corporate names may be trademarks or registered trademarks, and are used only for identification and explanation without intent to infringe.

*Library of Congress Cataloging-in-Publication Data*
A catalog record for this title has been requested

ISBN: 978-1-032-04056-1 (hbk)
ISBN: 978-1-032-04055-4 (pbk)
ISBN: 978-1-003-19037-0 (ebk)

DOI: 10.4324/9781003190370

Typeset in Optima
by Deanta Global Publishing Services, Chennai, India

Access the Support Material: www.routledge.com/9781032040554

*To Kerry, Austun, Karly, and Courtney, for whom I toil …*

# Contents

| | |
|---|---|
| *Figures* | x |
| *Meet the Author* | xii |
| *Preface* | xiii |
| *Acknowledgments* | xviii |
| *Abbreviations* | xix |
| *Supplemental Downloads* | xx |

| | | |
|---|---|---|
| **1** | **So, What Kind of School Do We Want, Anyway?** | **1** |
| | Relationships: The Foundation of the Foundation | 10 |
| | Small Moments Matter | 13 |
| | Listening (Seriously) | 14 |
| | Speak Courageously and Supervise/Mentor with Respect and Care | 17 |
| | Naming Names | 18 |
| | Have Fun | 20 |
| | Display Appreciation | 22 |
| | Build Relationship Equity | 24 |
| | Listening 2.0 | 27 |
| | Messaging | 30 |
| | Pulling It All Together | 32 |
| | Summary | 33 |
| | References | 35 |
| **2** | **How Can Our Systems Support the Three Foundational Principles?** | **38** |
| | A Bit about Systems | 40 |
| | Systems Thinking in Schools | 44 |

Contents

|   |   |   |
|---|---|---|
| | Schedule Considerations for Functioning Systems | 45 |
| | A System of Empowering, Collaborative Teams | 48 |
| | Communications Systems in Support of the Three Foundational Principles | 56 |
| | School Improvement Planning in Support of the Three Foundational Principles | 58 |
| | Summary | 63 |
| | References | 65 |
| **3** | **The Power of "Seeing It": The Collegial Visit** | **67** |
| | The Case for Teachers to Learn from One Another's Work | 69 |
| | Collegial Visits: *What?* | 75 |
| | Collegial Visits: *How?* | 76 |
| | Determining the Foci for Collegial Visits | 78 |
| | Determining the Collegial Visits Unit of Analysis and Team | 80 |
| | Creating Guiding Questions | 82 |
| | Creating the Space for Collegial Visits | 84 |
| | Facilitating the Visit: Immersing Teachers in the Work | 87 |
| | Facilitating the Debriefing Session: Where Learning Connections Are Made | 87 |
| | Summary | 88 |
| | References | 91 |
| **4** | **Building a Teacher Leadership System** | **96** |
| | Why Your School Needs Teacher Leadership | 98 |
| | Demystifying Leadership for Teachers | 103 |
| | Teacher Leadership by the Standards | 107 |
| | Fostering Teacher Leadership Formally: *The Teacher Leadership Academy* | 107 |
| | Who Should Participate? | 111 |
| | How Can We Recruit Teacher Leaders? | 112 |
| | Teacher Leadership Academy: *How?* and *What?* | 114 |
| | Selecting Teacher Leadership Projects | 117 |
| | Celebrating Teacher Leaders' Work | 120 |
| | Summary | 121 |
| | References | 122 |

| 5 | **Amplifying Teacher Leadership beyond the School's Walls** | **126** |
|---|---|---|
| | Why Consider Teacher Leadership beyond the School? | 129 |
| | Leadership and Sharing at the District Level | 130 |
| | Advocacy and Sharing beyond the District Level | 132 |
| | *Testifying at a Public Hearing* | 133 |
| | *Educational Organizations* | 134 |
| | *Presenting Your Successes* | 136 |
| | *Writing for Publication* | 139 |
| | *Seeking Outside Funding* | 142 |
| | Goal Setting for Future Leadership Efforts | 144 |
| | Summary | 145 |
| | References | 147 |

*Glossary*   149

# Figures

| | | |
|---|---|---|
| 1.1 | The three foundational principles to empower teacher leadership | 6 |
| 1.2 | Would Teachers Rather? A quick screener to determine the level of empowerment, collegiality, and risk taking in your school | 9 |
| 1.3 | Appreciation audit and enhancement tool | 24 |
| 1.4 | Relationship equity with diminishers and enhancers | 25 |
| 1.5 | Questions to assess your relationship-equity-building skills in everyday interactions | 26 |
| 1.6 | Participative leadership inquiries | 28 |
| 1.7 | Problem solver versus problem identifier tool | 29 |
| 2.1 | The three foundational principles to empower teacher leadership | 40 |
| 2.2 | Systems thinking questions for schools | 46 |
| 2.3 | Generic schedule with common planning time for four teachers for one school day | 47 |
| 2.4 | Key teams to support empowerment, collegiality, and risk taking | 49 |
| 2.5 | Sample team connections map | 50 |
| 2.6 | Sample purpose statement for Instructional Leadership Team | 52 |
| 2.7 | Team system analysis | 55 |
| 2.8 | Sample minutes template for a team meeting | 57 |
| 2.9 | Team communication planning worksheet | 58 |
| 2.10 | Sample school improvement action plan template | 60 |
| 2.11 | School improvement plan (SIP) timeline to maximize engagement and support the three foundational principles | 62 |
| 3.1 | The three foundational principles to empower teacher leadership | 77 |
| 3.2 | Potential foci for collegial visits | 80 |

| | | |
|---|---|---|
| 3.3 | Sample set of generalizable guiding questions for a round of collegial visits | 83 |
| 3.4 | Sample note-taking template for collegial visits with an unspecified focus | 84 |
| 3.5 | Sample collegial visits memo with rotating coverage model | 86 |
| 3.6 | Protocol for collegial visit debriefing meetings with sample language | 89 |
| 4.1 | The three foundational principles to empower teacher leadership | 99 |
| 4.2 | Teacher leadership reflective questions | 105 |
| 4.3 | Summary of the Teacher Leader Model Standards | 108 |
| 4.4 | Recruitment messages for a teacher leadership academy | 113 |
| 4.5 | Potential elements in a teacher leadership academy (TLA) application | 115 |
| 4.6 | Potential teacher leadership academy professional learning foci | 117 |
| 4.7 | Teacher leadership academy project proposal template | 118 |
| 4.8 | Possible teacher leadership academy projects | 120 |
| 5.1 | The three foundational principles to empower teacher leadership | 128 |
| 5.2 | Recommendations for Board of Education presentations by school leadership teams | 131 |
| 5.3 | Generic template for public testimony | 134 |
| 5.4 | Sample public testimony in support of a powerful, though fictitious, bill | 135 |
| 5.5 | Considerations for educational presentations | 138 |
| 5.6 | Considerations for publication | 141 |
| 5.7 | Considerations for grant writing | 144 |
| 5.8 | Leadership goal-setting worksheet | 145 |

# Meet the Author

Jeremy D. Visone is a faculty member in the Department of Educational Leadership, Policy & Instructional Technology at Central Connecticut State University (CCSU). In addition to preparing graduate students who are aspiring educational leaders, Jeremy also serves as the Partnership Liaison to public school districts, and he is the Coordinator of the Internship in Educational Leadership. His research interests include teacher leadership, collaborative structures for teachers, equity, teacher evaluation, developing problem-solving skills for aspiring educational leaders, and the practices of U.S. National Blue Ribbon Schools. Prior to his work at CCSU, Jeremy was a building leader at the elementary and secondary levels, most recently serving as the proud principal of Anna Reynolds Elementary School in Newington, Connecticut, which was named a U.S. National Blue Ribbon School in 2016.

When not focusing on teaching and research, Jeremy can be found at the gym lifting weights and finding other means to be active. Jeremy lives in Cromwell, Connecticut, with his wife, Kerry, and their three, sometimes cooperative children.

Jeremy enjoys connecting with readers of his works. Be encouraged to contact him at visone@ccsu.edu to discuss how the ideas in this book have resonated in your setting!

# Preface

At times, in education, we are told that this program, this method, and this way, is *the* way to see success. I will not attempt to convince you that there is one path to a successful school. Conversely, I subscribe to the notion that the business of leading schools is so complex and context specific that any linear and/or simplistic approach is practically guaranteed to fail. In this book, I will share with you many strategies and systems that have worked for me and others whose leadership I have studied or with whom I have worked. These ideas are also supported by the ever-expanding universe of literature in our field about effective leadership. This text is not so much a recipe or procedure for a science lab, with its concrete sequence of steps to follow, as it is a "choose your own adventure" book. You must determine how the ideas I share align with your context and the climate in your school. My hope is to offer all my readers a series of ideas that, when applied as applicable in your schools, will move you closer to where you want to be.

I have been incredibly fortunate to work alongside so many outstanding educators from whom I have learned so much. As such, many of the ideas here belong not to me but to the profession. The individuals are far too numerous to outline here, and I will introduce you to a small number of them throughout this book. I would be remiss not to specifically acknowledge the Newington (CT) Public Schools, where I worked for many years and with which I continue to partner, and the Cromwell (CT) Public Schools, with which I continue to partner. Within these two districts, I have learned so much of what is presented here. In Newington, I served in roles ranging from substitute teacher to principal, and I was able to learn by doing at John Wallace Middle School and Anna Reynolds Elementary School. I observed how so many other great leaders operated, and I emulated their craft and tweaked their ideas to apply them in my own setting. This formative education was invaluable, and I owe much to the district and its wonderful students and educators. I treasure my time there and aim to pay forward my learning to others, particularly through our expanding partnership work. In Cromwell, I have applied my knowledge of leadership to partnership work between my institution, Central Connecticut State University, and the district. We have operated our Teacher Leadership Academy there since 2017, and the teacher leaders' work, over these years, has been impressive and inspiring. Again, I had the opportunity to learn by doing, and I share the fruits of this opportunity herein.

This text developed over the last three years, after hearing my leadership students continually ask how to accomplish the leadership aims that we discussed. Theory is helpful and always thought provoking, but my students have always craved the next step: how to apply the theory to their school contexts. In other words, *how do we actually do this?* It is this next step that I have attempted to recreate here. Some of this work is not glamorous (No one who knows me would *ever* accuse me of being glamorous!); nor is it particularly radical. The ideas presented here are practical, and they are easily adaptable to the contexts of your specific situation. The hope is that you will find some (or *all*—it would be totally fine with me if everything resonated with you!) of these ideas worthy of application to your context.

When I was a principal, I espoused a value that you will read about repeatedly throughout this text. Namely, teachers should see themselves as leaders. They should feel empowered to contribute to the leadership of the school. I used to assert, "Reynolds as leaders." Reynolds was short for Anna Reynolds, the former principal after whom our school was named, and the wording was shorthand for my expectation that all staff members should view and comport themselves as leaders. I needed their help to lead the school effectively. The staff at Anna Reynolds (and John Wallace) stepped up beyond my expectations, and I am so fortunate to have had the great pleasure of working with this dedicated and talented group of educators.

I am also so fortunate to work with aspiring educational leaders and teacher leaders. As a faculty member at a university that prepares educators at the graduate level for leadership roles, I have a permanent front-row seat to their tales of exemplary leadership, as well as the "nonexamples" displaying abject leadership failure. From my vantage point, I can assist teachers to develop a leadership point of view, whether they plan to be a principal or just the best darn colleague around. There are roles for all types of leaders in our schools, and our preK–12 students certainly need all these leaders to express their talents. Who am I talking to? I am talking to *you*. At a minimum, you likely have some leadership dispositions already, considering you have picked up this book, and you are probably interested in improving what you and your school do. After all, there are systems to be created, tweaked, and reimagined. Your students and colleagues are depending on your leadership to make their conditions that much more coherent, meaningful, and effective. Whatever your role, level of experience, or motivation, let's roll up our sleeves and get to work!

## Who Is This Book For?

The content in this book is designed for several different constituent groups in their work to improve their schools. For formal school leaders, this book provides strategies and ideas that you can consider for application. It provides you with strategies to cultivate a team approach to leading your school, which should render your efforts both less exhausting and more effective. This book offers specific ways to build your teachers' capacities for leadership, and it shares forums and practices that will put teachers in positions to express their leadership. For teachers, this book provides a competing vision to the traditional model of teaching your students and largely disregarding all else occurring in the school. You can expand your leadership perspectives to become a better colleague to other teachers, a more effective teacher to your students, a stronger advocate for all the school's students, and a materially helpful complement to your school's formal leaders—in other words, a *teacher leader*! For teachers aspiring to administrative roles, you likely wonder how to lead a school, and this book shares a vision of a collaborative, participative organization that is transformative in its process, via the efforts of a strong team. For those leading graduate courses of study for teachers, this book provides ample material for discussion about who should serve as leaders within schools and how. It is my hope that this book can provoke thought for educators across many job titles and settings.

## What To Expect in This Book

The book is organized into five chapters. Chapter 1 introduces three foundational principles—*empowerment*, *collegiality*, and *risk taking*, which serve

Preface

as the touchstones for all the strategies and systems presented in the book. Chapter 1 also presents foundations for a school that values teacher leadership. Not surprisingly, these foundations are heavily influenced by interpersonal relationships. This chapter will explore the relational conditions that underlie any effective application of ideas that follow in later chapters. Though the process of empowering teacher leadership is not a linear one, overall, it is my view that a professional school culture, beginning with productive interpersonal relationships, precedes any meaningful effort to improve teacher leadership at scale. I implore leaders of all types to afford these foundations the attention they deserve.

Chapter 2 outlines logistical considerations for building a team structure that includes teacher leadership. These considerations include scheduling, team systems, communication, and school improvement. Chapter 3 introduces a means, *collegial visits*, for teachers to learn from one another through the common viewing of peers' instruction. In essence, your school can leverage one of its greatest resources—*its teachers*—as a renewable and empowering source of professional learning. Chapter 4 shares ways to cultivate teacher leadership strategically and systematically through a dedicated *teacher leadership academy*. Through a teacher leadership academy, motivated teachers can experience professional learning, benefit from conversations with like-minded colleagues, and lead projects of value to both themselves and their schools. Finally, Chapter 5 applies teacher leadership beyond the scope of your school. Ideas are provided so teachers can share their successes and learning with others through presentation, publications, and participation in educational organizations. As stated earlier, this book does not provide a linear, formulaic approach to developing teacher leadership. Rather, many aspects of this complex work are shared, and you can work with your team to find the application to your school.

## Special Features

Various special features are included to assist you with accessing the book's content. Each chapter begins with a short vignette to present real-world challenges related to the chapter's content. Though the names and places are pseudonyms, the situations and issues raised are all based on the realities of contemporary schools. I have no doubt you will relate to much of what you read in these situations! Within the body of each chapter, there

# Preface

are numerous figures that include information to enhance the text, examples of the chapter's content in practice, and tools your team can use to analyze your school. Many of the tools are also available as downloadable, editable files via the book's eResources collection, which can be accessed here: www.routledge.com/9781032040554. In addition, each chapter concludes with a series of questions for consideration, which can help you to process the chapter's content and push your thinking further.

# Acknowledgments

Figures 2.5 and 2.6 are adapted from "We can do this! Transformational leadership for school improvement," by J. D. Visone (in press), in K. N. LaVenia & J. J. May (Eds.), *Case Studies in Leadership and Adult Development: Applying Theoretical Perspectives to Real World Challenges*. Routledge. Adapted with permission.

# Abbreviations

| | |
|---|---|
| **PLC** | professional learning community |
| **SEL** | social and emotional learning |
| **SIP** | school improvement plan |
| **SMART** | strategic/specific, measurable, attainable, results-based, and timebound |
| **STEM** | science, technology, engineering, and mathematics |
| **TED** | technology, entertainment, and design |
| **TLA** | teacher leadership academy |
| **TLFP** | teacher leader fellowship program |
| **TSE** | teacher self-efficacy |

# Supplemental Downloads

Some of the tools in this book can be downloaded and printed for use in your schools. You can access these downloads by visiting the book product page on our website, www.routledge.com/9781032040554. Then click on the tab that says Support Material and select the files.

## eResource Page

- Figure 1.2 Would Teachers Rather? A quick screener to determine the level of empowerment, collegiality, and risk taking in your school.
- Figure 1.3 Appreciation audit and enhancement tool.
- Figure 2.7 Team system analysis.
- Figure 2.8 Sample minutes template for a team meeting.
- Figure 2.9 Team communication planning worksheet.
- Figure 2.10 Sample school improvement action plan template.
- Figure 3.4 Sample note-taking template for collegial visits with an unspecified focus.
- Figure 4.7 Teacher leadership academy project proposal template.
- Figure 5.8 Leadership goal-setting worksheet.

# So, What Kind of School Do We Want, Anyway?

"What is the point of this?" Greta muttered to herself, as her principal, Theodore, droned on about another initiative affecting the Language Arts department at Status Quo High School. The initiative—increasing the rigor of student work through examining the cognitive level of questions and learning activities—was surely connected to researched-based practice. Greta deduced this fact, based upon Theodore's presentation, but she did not understand the connection between this work and the larger school goals, which she thought she remembered related to improving students' SAT scores and the statewide accountability index score for the school. Further, she whispered under her breath to Evan, a department colleague who taught some of the same courses, "My classes are hard enough—I have about 10% of my kids failing each semester. If I make things any more difficult, I will just have to give too many Fs!"

Evan chuckled without probing Greta's comments further, and Greta returned her attention to her cellphone, scrolling through emails and checking text messages from the day, while she listened half-heartedly to Theodore's presentation. She had seen how the content of these professional "learning" sessions resulted in little actual learning, few classroom instructional changes, and even less follow through from administrators. Thus, she could afford to give this initiative perfunctory attention, until it went away. "Who is doing the work during your lessons? And how much cognitive load are your students exerting with a task that only asks them to describe something?" Theodore asked the group.

Blah, blah, blah. I need to think about what I am teaching tomorrow, and, oh yeah, I need to plan to lead our data team meeting tomorrow, too! Ugh. Greta thought to herself. She wished silently that Theodore would

DOI: 10.4324/9781003190370-1

adjourn the meeting early, so she could plan for tomorrow and get home earlier.

After the meeting, Greta drove home, focusing her thoughts on the next phase of her day, which included preparing dinner for her family after a short stint at the gym, where she could work off her stress. Looking back upon her day at Status Quo High, she saw a department where each teacher, even those who were teaching the same courses, operated as an independent actor. Yes, Greta was the appointed leader of her data team, where she, Evan, and the other three teachers of Grade 9 English met to discuss assessments, curriculum, and whatever other disconnected work the administrators decided to throw at them. However, she did not really know how her colleagues taught, nor did she recognize the value of knowing this information, as she believed her pedagogy was just fine the way it was.

At the data team meeting the next day, Greta inquired, "Who has the preassessment data about literary devices?" Three of the five data team members responded affirmatively.

One of the others, Thomas, stated, "Sorry about that. I have gotten a bit behind in the curriculum, and I was not ready to administer it."

The other was Geradine, who commented, "I really don't care for that assessment. I'd rather use another one I used in the past. Anyway, I can predict for you that my kids will be terrible with literary devices. They always are, every year, and this group is as low as ever!"

With only some data available, the group had a general conversation about the students' gaps with respect to the topic of literary devices, and they then shifted to the more motivating inquiry from Greta of "How should we teach literary devices?" From this inquiry, the group brainstormed ideas, which were individually described and endorsed by the teachers. With little commentary or evaluation of the pedagogical merit of any of the approaches, the conversation trailed off on its own, and the group was left to determine, by teacher, how instruction in the unit would progress. Greta did not care for the style of her colleague, Evan, who was much more "loose" in his teaching style, following many student-identified pathways and differentiating products by choice and ability. Greta found his approach to be too much to manage, and these ideas conflicted with her "tried and true" methods.

Not surprisingly, when the post assessment results were examined weeks later at another data team meeting, there was a wide range of achievement across classes (from 67% to 95% mastery of the literary devices standards

## What Kind of School Do We Want, Anyway?

for the unit). The main explanation given for the discrepancy around the table was that the higher-scoring classes had more capable students. After all, the administrators created classes that were not equitable, in the teachers' minds, and this perspective was one that was continually referenced as a rationale for less-than-optimal student performance. After explaining away the range of mastery, the group decided to turn their attention to the next unit of study.

The only time in the week where the teachers shared or collaborated was during these 45-minute data team meetings. Not surprisingly, Status Quo High had not seen much growth in student achievement for decades. Many students were successful, but many were not. Teacher morale was low, and there was a general mistrust of administration. Knowing these characteristics of her school, Greta aimed to spend as little of her time at work and, by extension, with her colleagues, as possible.

Is Status Quo High School *your* school? Okay, I am not looking to embarrass anyone. Let's say that it is the school of a "friend." There is no judgment here. In reality, this anecdote aligns with the experience of so many educators across the United States. Many teachers work in environments where compliance is a more prevailing norm than true collaboration and problem solving. It is not uncommon to hear teachers speak about how initiatives will fall by the wayside, as new ones come along, and many schools suffer from the low or stagnant achievement that accompanies poor staff morale and lack of trust in the administration. Teachers frequently cannot see the connections among what they discuss at their data team meetings, what they learn during professional learning experiences, and what they planned for their lesson tomorrow.

However, the more important question to ask here is: *Is this the kind of school I want?* If you answer my inquiry with an enthusiastic:

> Yes! Self, this is exactly the kind of place I want to work—one where I do what I have to do to meet the minimum requirements; one where I can spend the least amount of time and expend the least amount of effort; one where colleagues and supervisors will not expect too much of me and will never hold me accountable for what I do and don't do; one where I don't really value my administrators as instructional leaders; and one where I don't feel much connection to colleagues or their work!

then please, *by all means,* STOP READING THIS BOOK!

Put a different way, if you are not interested in collaboration, empowerment, risk taking, and, thus, transformation of practice for the benefit of students, then this book will be a *complete waste of your time*! I hate wasting people's time, so I figured I would give you an out after the first couple of pages.

However, for those of you who wish to do better—for those who aspire to create a school culture that is empowering, collaborative, and safe for pedagogical risk taking, then this book is designed to help you move the needle in this direction, whether you are a formal school leader, such as an administrator with a title, or an informal one, such as a dedicated and caring teacher, who wants to help lead your colleagues to a more successful place. That's right. I am talking to you. No, not the person behind you. *You*. In this book, I will reference "leadership" often, and I am referring to all administrators, teachers, and school community members who can contribute to making your school stronger. This book is about purposefully building a team leadership disposition and structure. In addition, aside, perhaps, from the nominal cost of purchasing of this book, the methods and systems described herein are the type that a former superintendent of mine would say meet the demands of "using existing resources." That, my fellow educators, is a euphemism for doing better with not one red cent more.

Furthermore, the most important resource you need for this type of work is already housed within your school. No, I am not referring to those new teacher laptops with lightning-fast processors—though they will be most useful, too. I am not even writing about the digital learning platform you use to connect with students remotely. Your biggest resource is the *people* who will do the work—the formal leaders, teachers, and support staff (Sterrett, 2015). In my work to prepare practicing teachers to become educational leaders, I spend much time in and around schools. A select few of these schools are wildly successful in terms of student achievement. Most others are in a flattened pattern of stagnation, where some students achieve and others generally don't. Still other schools' levels of student achievement could be described as falling somewhere between "on life support" and "dumpster fire."

However, something all these schools have in common is that they all have dedicated and capable teachers within their walls. You all know who these "roving leaders" are. Formal leaders can count on them to support leadership efforts and what the school is, collectively, attempting to accomplish. They are working for students and their success, and they generally

## What Kind of School Do We Want, Anyway?

get the best results. They are the least likely to take all their allotted days off, and they spend much of their own time preparing for their superior instruction. If you are a fellow teacher, you know who these special teachers are, too. They are the people you go to when you need a piece of advice. If you are reading this book with intention, there is a good chance that *you* are one of these teacher leaders, too. No doubt, different schools will have varying percentages of the teacher leaders I have described, but, each school, invariably, has some of them. And this is the starting point for your trajectory toward greatness. With a dedicated, collegial core of like-minded individuals, your school can begin a journey to become a more collaborative, empowering, and risk-friendly learning environment for all, students and staff, alike. The burning question you are likely wrestling with is: *How can we get there?* I'm so glad you asked!

First, I will introduce you to three, simple principles that, when espoused often—and, more importantly, *practiced with regularly*—will move your school toward the type of ideal work environment described above. These guiding principles will be referenced continually throughout this book, as these principles serve as the frame of reference for all the strategies and logistics shared. The principles are:

(a) **empowerment**: Our staff members feel competent and believe that they are equipped to make decisions in the best interest of our students and school. Our teachers have sound ideas that can improve what we do;

(b) **collegiality**: Our staff works together to solve problems of practice. We do not work in isolation. What we learn, we share; and,

(c) **risk taking**: We do not advance if we do not try new things and experiment. We are not afraid to do things differently.

Figure 1.1 shows the three principles in a more compact and, perhaps, aesthetically pleasing format.

When I was a principal, I shared these three principles at the first and last faculty meetings each year. My purpose was to ensure our staff knew what I valued. That was the easy part. The hard part was making sure to consistently live these values during daily interactions with teachers in the context of our complicated work. For example, I could not espouse empowerment in a whole-group setting and then regularly tell teachers that they could not have input into decision making in the school. Luckily, a system of teams

| | |
|---|---|
| **empowerment** | Our staff members feel competent and believe that they are equipped to make decisions in the best interest of our students and school. Our teachers have sound ideas that can improve what we do. |
| **collegiality** | Our staff works together to solve problems of practice. We do not work in isolation. What we learn, we share. |
| **risk taking** | We do not advance if we do not try new things and experiment. We are not afraid to do things differently. |

*Figure 1.1* The three foundational principles to empower teacher leadership.

can be leveraged to make empowerment come alive and have concrete, tangible meaning for teachers. This systems approach is the work of Chapter 2. In terms of collegiality, I needed to make sure that, if I expected teachers to work together, I actually provided them a time and space to do so (*Duh!*). Setting up systems for teacher collaboration will be addressed in Chapters 2 and 3. Lastly, if a teacher came to me with an innovative way of teaching that was a bit outside the box, I needed to have some comfort with this concept and offer support, within reason. If the strategy didn't work, as evidenced by student data, then we would abandon it, but, if it *did* work, we had identified a practice worth replicating! However, the key to risk taking is creating safety in trying something different. After all, we never get anywhere different than where we are if we continue to always do what we always have done. (*Try saying that ten times fast!*) Creating professional safety for staff that supports collegiality, innovation, and risk taking is the primary work of this chapter.

These three guiding principles are supported by literature on effective school leadership. A justification for teacher empowerment can be found within the *professional capital* framework of Andy Hargreaves and Michael Fullan (2012, 2013). Though this framework will be explored more fully in Chapter 3, its relevance here is noteworthy. First, one element of the professional capital framework is *decisional capital*, which refers to teachers' ability to make sound decisions that are informed by their experiences and learning, often from each other. In order to maximize the value of decisional capital, teachers must, within reason, be allowed to make decisions for their own students and more broadly in the school. This freedom is agency and empowerment. In my own research on some of the most effective schools in the United States (Visone, 2018), empowerment conditions, including leadership trust in teachers, a pattern of valuing teacher input, and providing opportunities for teacher decision making were evident and self-espoused leverage points for these schools' successes.

Some of the most successful schools in the world can be found in Finland, where results in recent years have been touted as exemplary when compared to other nations. Authors Pasi Sahlberg and Timothy Walker share some glimpses into this success in their recent work *In Teachers We Trust: The Finnish Way to World-Class Schools*. They explain that, in Finland, teachers are well-respected in society, and teachers are, as the book title implies, entrusted to make pedagogical decisions. Further, connecting to the second guiding principle I shared above, Finnish schools emphasize teacher collaboration (Sahlberg & Walker, 2021).

It is likely not a huge intellectual leap to understand the value of collegiality in school success. By collegiality, I mean a set of dispositions and actions that are the hallmarks of true collaboration. These include a willingness to learn from one another, an inclination to work together to solve problems of practice, and a sharing mindset. The professional capital framework includes a construct called *social capital*, which is defined by the authors as the totality of interactions between teachers (Hargreaves & Fullan, 2012, 2013). As will be outlined in Chapter 3, students learn more when their teachers learn together and from each other (Leana, 2011). In order to meet the many challenges presented to teachers and leaders, educators need to collaborate to leverage their collective power to accomplish more (Drago-Severson & Blum-DeStefano, 2018). The result is a school that is more than the sum of its parts.

Risk taking is the least studied and understood of the three principles (Howard et al., 2018). Often, a fear of failure and risk aversion can prevent a school from innovating and moving forward (Fullan & Kirtman, 2019). However, consider that we educators expect students to be risk takers in the classroom. We exhort students to raise their hands, even when they are unsure if their answers are correct, and we tell students to exhibit growth mindsets by trying things outside their comfort zones—and even *making mistakes*—in order to learn new things. If we seek these dispositions in students, adults should model them. Further, as Howard et al. (2018) determined when interviewing teachers, the experience of risk taking allows for the possibility of changing the way one teaches and, therefore, improvement of practice.

By focusing on the three foundational principles (empowerment, collegiality, and risk taking), leaders across all types of roles can help unlock the potential within your school. Thus, it would be informative to determine where your school stands now, with respect to their prevalence. Figure 1.2 is an exercise to help you determine this information. Think of it as a G-rated, educator version of the oft-inappropriate game *Would you rather?* you might have played as a youngster (or last week at happy hour). When using this tool, try to account for what teachers *actually do*, as opposed to what they say they will do, as we all know that people's actions do not always match their espoused values. An editable and printable version of this screener can be found in the eResources collection for this book.

Depending on the score you calculated from the *Would teachers rather?* screener, you might proceed with this book differently. For example, schools in the least empowering, collegial, and risk-taking category (0–4 points) should spend much time and energy in the foundations for this work, which are found in Chapter 1, since your deficits are likely cultural. For those in the middle category (5–7 points), the logistics found in Chapters 2, 3, and 4 might be the most helpful to provide some new ideas to capitalize on your adequate foundation. Just a structure or system (or two) might be missing or need attention to help move your school forward. Schools in the highest category of function (8–10 points) could benefit, in particular, from the leadership participation beyond the school discussed in Chapter 5 to enrich your work and push your leadership to the next level, though there will likely be some ideas and strategies in all chapters that can enhance your solid foundation.

No matter where your school falls on the scoring guide, for those who are "all in" to build an effective and efficient team that works together for a common cause—improved student learning—read on. Herein, you will examine means of incrementally turning the cultural tide of professionalism in the right direction—from relationship building, to modeling, to espoused values, to systems creation, to specific strategies to learn from each other, to explicitly building teacher leadership, to leading beyond your school. Since education is so dependent on relationships, we will begin with the importance of getting professional relationships right. Do not fall into the trap of underestimating the importance of the relationships all members of your team build and maintain. You might think the relationship content presented in this chapter is so basic that it needs not be reviewed. However, I would argue that the mentality of minimizing the importance of the "little stuff" of professional relationships has failed many schools. Attention to the important details of relationship building will set you on a course toward meaningful improvement.

## What Kind of School Do We Want, Anyway?

**Directions:** *Select one answer choice for each item based upon what you believe a majority of teachers in the school would choose (not necessarily how you, personally, would choose).* Then add all the points accumulated in the "1" column for a total score, and write that score in the box below that column. Compare your total score to the scoring guide below.

| Would teachers rather . . .   Points | 0 | 1 |
|---|---|---|
| 1. create lesson plans independently or with their teaching peers? | Independently | Peers |
| 2. have administration hand them an already-created preassessment or create one? | Receive | Create |
| 3. solve a curricular problem independently or with teaching peers? | Independently | Peers |
| 4. use existing teaching methods for efficiency or try something new that has been shown by others to be effective? | Existing | New |
| 5. avoid making a pedagogical mistake or take a pedagogical risk to possibly get better results? | Avoid Mistake | Take Risk |
| 6. proceed without an answer or ask an administrator for assistance? | Proceed | Ask the Admin |
| 7. use data teams to solve problems that are posed by administrators or their teams? | Administrators | Teams |
| 8. have each team member independently conduct his or her own research to find a way to solve a pedagogical dilemma or watch a colleague teach who has a possible solution? | Independent Own Research | Watch Colleague |
| 9. examine data for their own students, only, or for all students across their entire grade, department, or school? | Own Students Only | All Students |
| 10. ask administration to solve problems or try to solve the problems alongside administration? | Administration Only | Solve Alongside |
| | **Total Score:** | |

**Scoring Guide:**
0-4 = Needs A Lot of Work (Isolationist); 5-7 = Not Bad, but Can Improve (Emergent); 8-10 = Has a Solid Foundation Established (Established)

*Figure 1.2* Would Teachers Rather? A quick screener to determine the level of empowerment, collegiality, and risk taking in your school.

##  Relationships: The Foundation of the Foundation

In their critically important work, *School Leadership That Works: From Research to Results*, Robert Marzano, Timothy Waters, and Brian McNulty (2005) outlined the *21 Responsibilities of the School Leader*, which is a meta-analysis-generated accounting of behaviors and roles of effective administrators. In other words, what do effective educational leaders do to influence student achievement? This framework is incredibly useful to those concerned with school leadership, and I will reference it multiple times throughout this work. Here, we focus on the authors' recognition that an effective school leader must cultivate positive personal relationships with other staff members. This is not to say that administrators should be looking to befriend those they lead. However, a respectful, professional relationship that is based upon trust and mutual admiration is desired. In some of my own research with U.S. National Blue Ribbon Schools (Visone, 2018), which are recognized by their states as highly effective at either: (a) overall student achievement or (b) closing achievement gaps, I found that these highly effective schools espoused trusting relationships between teachers and administrators as foundational and important in creating a base from which effective pedagogical work could be built.

Continuing with the construction analogy, psychologist Abraham Maslow (1970) provided us the theoretical support for necessitating trusting relationships with his pyramid-shaped model of human needs. On the second-most-foundational layer of the pyramid (just above physiological needs, such as food, shelter, and water—not to be underestimated if you have attempted to host a professional learning workshop without food or in a room that is too cold or hot!), we find safety needs. Safety, though traditionally considered from a physical security standpoint, also applies to leadership culture in schools through the safety of ideas and livelihood. In other words, if teachers fear that their leaders and colleagues are seeking to catch them making a mistake or, worse yet, actively trying to terminate their employment or compete against them, creativity and risk taking will be at a minimum. The emotion of fear saps energy from what the team is trying to accomplish, leaving little left for the tasks at hand (Sinek, 2014). Further, as Maslow (1970) asserted, advancing to higher levels on the pyramid is impossible without having met the levels of need below. Thus, the teacher who cannot take a pedagogical risk will not feel a part of the team, since she has not yet checked off the safety box, and belonging needs are higher up the chain. Without the psychological safety of the staff, leaders will accomplish little and have difficulty challenging the status quo (Fullan & Kirtman, 2019). Educational consultant Robyn Jackson even went so far as to identify a lack of psychological safety and risk taking for teachers as signs of a toxic school (Jackson, as cited in Epitropoulos, 2019), indicating what can happen when safety needs are ignored. You will logically ask in response: *But, Jeremy, how can leadership meet safety needs for staff members?*

Well-known management theorist Simon Sinek provided us more specific insight into how this occurs during his influential TED talk entitled *Why Good Leaders Make You Feel Safe* (Sinek, 2014). The short response to his inquiry is: *duh, because safety works*! But Sinek was also able to unpack the underlying mechanisms.

Sinek logically argued that the environment created by leaders—again, this would apply to *all* leaders, both those with titles and those without—greatly influences the capacity of the group to achieve. Within a very trusting environment, greatness can occur. However, he emphasized that, since trust is a feeling, an emotion, it cannot simply be transferred by espousing the right messages. Yes, our words are important, but how many times have we heard leaders say "Trust me!" only to have our hopes dashed by broken promises?

Instead, trust is built in the face of adversity that helps to mold the team into a unit that relies on its leaders for direction and support. Consider the many outside forces that impact a school: societal expectations, pressures to increase student achievement, parental demands, socioeconomic challenges, budgetary constraints, etc. Leaders help to maintain the group's focus on that which is controllable from inside the walls of the school. This means sustaining teachers' attention on teaching and learning and our goals for improvement. This ability for leadership to keep the team focused on what we can control and what is really important is consistent with what Marzano et al. (2005) referred to as *discipline*. It is through the experience of adversity, through dealing with the myriad, complex challenges that face schools today, that leaders have opportunities to sacrifice of themselves for the benefit of the group. A leader might sacrifice extra time to deal with a problem, or "take one for the team" by apologizing for something out of the leader's actual control on behalf of the school, or, perhaps, complete non-instructional tasks (i.e. investigating a disciplinary situation) for colleagues to allow them to do the more important work of teaching kids. All these examples are daily ways formal and informal leaders can show their colleagues that they are leading from alongside them and not always from the front.

Once a leader has shown her willingness to sacrifice for the benefit of teachers, trust is built, and safety is the prevailing norm. This, Sinek (2014) asserted, is where greatness can occur. He noted that, when we feel safe, we will work together and harder. Individuals' natural reactions to safety are to trust and cooperate and help leadership meet its vision. I was purposeful not to use the term "principal" in this section because the feeling of safety can emanate as easily from the sacrifices of a teaching colleague, who contributes much extra work to allow a data team to operate smoothly, or the school psychologist, who makes the phone call home for a classroom teacher about a student experiencing significant behavioral challenges. Good leadership can be found up and down the roles of the most effective schools, and trust within the group is the responsibility of all team members.

Beyond exhibiting sacrifice for your staff or colleagues, there are other concrete ways to build positive, trusting relationships. Consider the *five facets of trust* framework, as outlined by Tschannen-Moran and Gareis (2015). They identified vulnerability, benevolence, honesty, openness, and competence as ways that leaders, principals in their analysis, can engender trust among their staff. I will expand the logic to apply to leaders in all roles. Vulnerability aids in building trust in a reciprocal fashion. For example, leaders must recognize the vulnerable position teachers, students, and parents occupy and respect this position by protecting these groups' interests at all times. It is not acceptable, for example, to widely share issues of personal significance (i.e. disability status, health conditions, personal strife, pedagogical challenges, etc.). This applies as much to teaching peers as it does to formal leaders. In the reverse direction, leaders should display their own vulnerability to those they lead by espousing that they trust others to make decisions, consistent with the Finnish model outlined by Sahlberg and Walker (2021). If vulnerability is displayed in both directions, stakeholders can experience opportunities to build trust.

Benevolence involves leadership behaviors that display care and concern for others. School leaders will frequently be called upon to make decisions in the face of challenging situations (i.e. student discipline, personal tragedies, personnel discord, etc.). Throughout all these situations, it is critical to consider individuals' humanity and try to create solutions that come from a position of caring for others' welfare. There are infinite moments as educators when we are given chances to express our benevolence. When we send a card and well wishes to a colleague who has lost a parent, or when a teacher helps a child who is hurt or sick, or when a leader assists a teacher with a child who has presented with academic difficulties, we meet the spirit of benevolence to help build others' trust in us.

Honesty and openness can be considered together. Honesty requires all leaders to tell the truth in all situations, which can serve as a manifestation of their integrity and authenticity. Relatedly, openness concerns leaders' transparency. Are leaders forthcoming with information, or are communications and answers vague and/or contradictory? Naturally, there are times when everyone cannot know all details of a situation (i.e. confidential health matters of colleagues, legal situations, etc.), but honesty and openness call upon leaders to speak transparently about circumstances when information must be withheld. Further, stating that a leader does not have an answer to a particular question is more honest and open than fabricating a response to extricate oneself from a conversation. Fellow educators are excellent judges of those in their midst who embellish, spin, or outright lie. Trust, logically, is not granted to these so-called leaders.

Finally, competence refers to leaders' ability to get a job done and do it well. Whether we are considering a principal creating a system that functions properly or a teacher leader delivering on a promise to provide colleagues with instructional resources to teach a common unit of study, competence is interconnected with follow through. He or she who follows through and is reliable is trusted.

## Small Moments Matter

First and foremost, allow me to ease the minds of those who do not enjoy public speaking. Contrary to what one might see on television or in the movies, the ability to build relationships and influence people's thoughts emanates not so much from grandiose soliloquies presented with Oscar-worthy delivery at a faculty meeting, department meeting, or professional learning workshop. Rather, it is within the small moments that trust is built among educators. It is certainly still important to publicly express that your office or classroom door is always open, that you can be trusted to help when others are in need, and/or that you value other's ideas. However, if the reality of this espoused accessibility is that you are most often behind closed doors, and you claim to be too busy to help others who have reached out to you for help, or you do not respond to emails with timely and meaningful replies, others will quickly conclude that your words are just that—*words*.

Recall the example shared earlier about the leader who announces, "Trust me!" We know that the proof is in the pudding, so to speak; leadership actions are what matter. For example, it is the situation where a colleague calls you at night to discuss something difficult, and you answer the call, listen, and offer sound advice that leads to a resolution, where true trust and respect are forged. It is the scenario when a teacher asks for your help with a difficult parental situation, and you provide a plan of action that results in the teacher improving the relationship with that parent, where you become a credible, trusted leader. Particularly for teacher leaders, it is during the fleeting hallway conversation, when a first-year teacher laments about a particular aspect of her instruction, and you promise to email her a particular resource—and you then follow through and do it!—resulting in her confidence increasing, where you build trust.

As the teacher leadership example illustrates, the importance of follow through cannot be overstated. Leaders who do what they say they will do will earn trust. Those who say they will do, and then always forget or do differently than they have said, will rightfully earn distrust and disappointment from those whose needs have not been met. Concretely, I implore all leaders to adopt a regular system to facilitate follow through. Are you a sticky note enthusiast? Do you send yourself emails as reminders? Do you set reminders on your phone or computer? If you are without pen and paper or—Heaven forbid!—your smart phone, will you ask teachers who have needs to simply email you with their requests, so you can be reminded of them later? It matters less what the system looks like, so long as it works to provide follow through and resolution to the myriad small moments that arise.

## Listening (Seriously)

How often have we seen interactions between parties (i.e. parents and administrators, teachers and administrators, students and teachers, etc.) become unproductive and negative due to a failure of each side to truly hear what the other side is saying? To proactively combat this all-too-familiar

## What Kind of School Do We Want, Anyway?

refrain, leaders in all roles need to model superior listening skills. In an informative *Educational Leadership* article, Brett Novick (2015) provided educational leaders with tips from a school counseling perspective. After all, counselors are adept at working with people during their worst moments. Perhaps, it is a child in crisis, family in disarray, teacher one ineffective lesson away from quitting teaching, etc. Counselors need to help diagnose problems via listening.

Novick first advised that leaders model active listening, which starts with doing more listening than speaking. Novick suggested letting the other individual speak first. Very often, someone who is upset really just needs to be heard, and your willingness to listen—without interruption, snippy retort, sarcasm, eye rolling, etc.—can display your empathy. Displaying your ability to view things from the other person's perspective, Novick asserted, might just be enough to resolve the situation, even if you cannot completely agree. Further, you provide yourself a chance to determine areas of commonality, no matter how infinitesimally minute they may be! If leaders always applied this practice, listening first and often, staff in your school would (a) feel heard and (b) see a model of how their own difficult interactions with students, parents, and (*gulp!*) other staff members should and could ensue. This advice is consistent with the time-honored guidance of Stephen Covey in his ubiquitous *The 7 Habits of Highly Effective People: Powerful Lessons in Personal Change* (2004). Covey implored us to listen with empathy so we can come to deeply know the problem and from where the other individual is coming. Covey shared a classic parable about a patient at the optometrist. The doctor tells the patient, who is having difficulty seeing clearly, to use the doctor's glasses. When the patient explains that the doctor's glasses make the problem even worse, the doctor myopically replies that the glasses have worked for him, so they should also work for the patient, as well. This type of poor listening skill—and subpar problem diagnosis—can lead to a lack of faith and trust in leadership. Further, a lack of listening on our part as leaders will lead to a proportionate lack of listening from those with whom we interact (Stone et al., 2010). If we want those we work alongside to hear our important messages, we need to model the listening we hope to earn in return.

Similarly, displaying interested body language, including eye contact, orienting toward the speaker, and remaining in proximity (as opposed to slowly creeping away mid-sentence), communicates to the speaker that her message will be heard and that you care. Sounds expert Julian Treasure, in his TED talk about listening (2011), provided some concrete steps to "consciously listen" via the acronym RASA. First, you must **r**eceive the information, which can only be done fully when leaders truly pay attention to the person speaking. Our body language referenced above can manifest our level of attention. Second, he shared that we need to **a**ppreciate the speaker, which entails making affirming noises, like "okay," "oh," and "yes." Again, body language can help here, as well, as nodding and smiling while maintaining eye contact can project an image of affirmation to the speaker. Next, is **s**ummarize, where an active listener can reflect back to the speaker what she believes she has heard. Responding "So, what I heard you say is …" is a concrete check for the speaker that her messages have been heard. Finally, Treasure suggested that empathic listeners **a**sk questions of the speaker. In order to deeply understand someone's perspective, as Covey suggested, we should be seeking clarity through follow-up questions. Efforts to understand others through intentional listening—often at the expense of expressing our own ideas—build the aforementioned trust and generate a sense of respect and value for others (Mieliwocki & Fatheree, 2019).

Further, one surefire way for your leadership team to develop credibility in the eyes of your stakeholders is to model and display a consistent dose of empathy. Though the scope of this book does not include an in-depth treatment of social and emotional learning (SEL), there is a relevant connection here. The Collaborative for Academic, Social, and Emotional Learning (CASEL) is a preeminent organization that advocates for the importance of SEL in schools. The relevance here is that you are trying to strengthen your team and create the type of trusting relationships necessary for excellence. According to CASEL (2013), SEL includes displaying empathy for others and establishing and maintaining positive relationships. Further, CASEL emphasizes that these skills are not only for students. Rather, the skills and dispositions developed through SEL can and should extend to the relationships among all stakeholders, which means you, too, adults! Further, for any SEL development to occur, the role of leadership to model and support SEL teachings is critical. Thus, for our purposes, if you desire teams and schools that consist of individuals who display empathy and develop the positive, trusting relationships needed for excellence, it starts with *you*. Every interaction. Every day. When you are feeling upset that others are not doing what you want or they are upset with you, start from a position of listening and work to understand their point of view.

## Speak Courageously and Supervise/Mentor with Respect and Care

All the aforementioned listening and empathy skills are put on display, in particular, during difficult conversations. Let's be honest. Not all leadership conversations or colleague interactions are positive and pleasant. At times, we need to share information with others that is unwelcome or difficult to hear. As a principal, you might need to inform a teacher that her practice does not meet expectations, *yet*. Or, as a teacher leader, you might need to tell a colleague that she is not following the established norms of your professional learning community. Perhaps a school leader needs to inform a parent that her request will not be honored. In any of these situations, active listening can be a powerful tool to combat emotions that can otherwise escalate the situation.

Covey (2004) recommended leaders aim for win–win outcomes, where the leader is prepared to agree to some of what the other person wants. Finding common ground is a concrete way to help both parties feel that they have moved forward.

Further, when working with teachers and discussing practice, the empathic leader or teacher leader colleague does not simply find fault, she offers a figurative hand. After all, it is feedback—and the delivery of that feedback—that is so important for growth. Certainly, entire books and courses of study are devoted to the supervision of teachers. A comprehensive discussion of this important leadership task is outside the scope of this work. However, I aim to plant dispositional seeds here. I want you to consider supervision as an *opportunity* to strengthen your team and contribute to your school's potential. Instead of saying, "That is not how we assess student learning here. I don't want to see you just lecturing and asking 'yes/no' questions," try something more like, "I noticed that you asked many 'yes/no' questions. Think about our recent professional learning about questioning. Let's craft some questions together that can raise the rigor level during your class discussions. You can use the question starters in this resource …" Better still, ask: "I noticed that you asked many 'yes/no' questions. What do you think about that?" This inquiry, depending on the teacher's response, can be followed by an offer to help.

If you are trying to move your school away from *I*, *me*, and *my* and toward *we*, *us*, and *our*, figuratively situate yourself, as a formal leader or teacher leader, right next to the teacher you are helping to improve her craft. This type of "We're in this together!" interaction manifests that the leader is invested, not in finding fault and catching teachers in making mistakes, but, rather, in teachers' growth. That is a powerful shift to make, and one that moves teachers away from the negativity and fear often associated with teacher evaluation (Donaldson, 2016). Of course, there is a time when tough talk is needed, such as when repeated attempts to help a struggling teacher have already been unsuccessful. However, most teacher supervision conversations can effectively follow a helpful pathway, and, when conversations are more supportive, and fear is not a factor, teachers will be more motivated for improvement (Fullan & Kirtman, 2019), as well as more receptive to constructive feedback.

Some of my own research with colleagues (Liu et al., 2019) has indicated that many teachers do not see value in the feedback they receive from leaders. Teachers want feedback that is grounded in evidence (i.e. relevant classroom interactions observed or based on student work) and connected to their professional learning. In Chapter 2, systems for supporting the three principles of empowerment, collegiality, and risk taking will help you to create coherence across the many facets of work within a school. Connecting supervision of teaching practice and professional learning is one inroad into this arena. Consider prompts like: "Since you did not get the results you expected, what do you want to know more about?" or "I think our team could use some professional learning in this area. Perhaps, we should seek out a conference or webinar. Are you interested in joining me, if I find one?"

In addition, if you, as a leader, model your own growth mindset and emphasize the formative aspect of supervision for your teachers and teammates, they will be less likely to fear the process. For example, don't be afraid to share when you earn a rating (i.e. for a goal, during an observation, etc.) that is below proficiency. Rather than displaying weakness in your practice, you affirm that no one is perfect or done learning, and you have a chance to model the proper mindset for your own learning that you likely want to see in your teachers or colleagues.

## Naming Names

It may seem insignificant and minor, but learning and using people's names is a gesture of respect. Now, some of you might be yelling at your books, saying, *But I am just so bad with names!* I retort simply, *Well, get good at them!* I am not suggesting that there are not some legitimate reasons for not knowing stakeholders' names, but a leader's inability to "name names" will be noticeable and disappointing to those you lead. They might ask themselves: *How can I trust this individual or buy into what he or she is asking of me when the person cannot take the time to learn my name?* I couldn't agree more. If you want to form a true team, all team members need to get to know the players on the team, from your night custodians, to your bus drivers, to your cafeteria workers, to your special education paraprofessionals—*everyone*. Further, once you all know the names, *use them* with regularity.

So, now you ask: *If you expect me to learn people's names, but I am not good at this skill, what can I do?* I am so glad you asked! The following are a few of my favorite strategies, which are based in brain research.

Allison Posey (2019), in her book, *Engage the Brain: How to Design for Learning That Taps into the Power of Emotion*, outlined many excellent strategies to help remember new information. First, Posey explained that our brain uses a "visual sketchpad" (p. 108) to recall visual relationships presented. We use this feature of our working memory when we spell words or figure our way around an unfamiliar school building after consulting a map. In the case of learning names of fellow staff members, the "visual sketchpad" can help us in some concrete ways. Try these visual strategies to learn those names:

- **create annotated lists** (i.e. with personal characteristics, interests, roles, etc.) of the people with whom you will interact;
- **study the photos** in your school's staff information system or your school's yearbook; or
- **create association webs**, where you make lists of people according to their roles and how they are related to each other.

A second component of working memory is the "phonological loop" (Posey, 2019, p. 111), which helps us to process sound input. This is where our conversations with others can come in handy. The more we converse with those whose names we wish to recall, the more likely we will be able to do so, which is another argument for the importance of social capital. Here are two more strategies to learn names that support our ability to retain auditorily accessed information and/or use our working memory:

- **verbally rehearse** names, including using alliteration (ex. Jovial Jeremy); or
- **verbally preview** individuals with whom you will interact at an upcoming meeting.

If you are skeptical and wonder how important this business of names is, consider the frequent feedback about the most beloved school administrators. Often, the first words of praise from a parent or staff member are something like: "She knew everyone." Further, consider that the consequences of not knowing names can include decreased quality of relationships and muted respect from those you wish to lead. As a new leader or colleague, people will be most impressed if you remember their name in your second meeting with them. Teachers share with me all the time that they are impressed by a new leader who seems to actually remember who they are and what they do. Be that leader or colleague. That means no more emails that begin with "Hi," without identifying the recipient. Start building that trust and professional community with this early, small gesture of respect.

## Have Fun

The work of educating children is complex and difficult. Sometimes, it can be downright exhausting, both mentally and physically. Given the demands and stresses associated with the job (i.e. curriculum pressures, accountability expectations, parental demands, etc.), it is important to find opportunities for fun and joy. Berg (2019) noted that reasons why many educators believe they should not have fun at work stem from the important moral imperative to teach all students; the current societal perception of teachers, who are constantly fighting negative attitudes about the rigor of their work; and the ubiquitous challenge of "not enough time." However, she specifically asserted that play "helps to promote and sustain a work climate that is positive and energized. It contributes to team building, risk taking, and increased trust" (p. 87). This perspective aligns completely with the aims of this chapter, which is focused on setting the foundation for building a team culture. Also, risk taking is one of the foundational principles, and Sinek (2014) taught us that teams function optimally under the umbrella of trust and safety.

Berg (2019) then shared ideas for mixing work and play, including activities during meetings that involve staff members generating metaphors, drawing visionary pictures, writing newspaper headlines to celebrate team accomplishments, and describing their emotions through emojis, to name a few. These strategies—using play-based, creative activities to accomplish work-related tasks—are vehicles to make the work seem less like a job and more like, well, *fun*.

I will extend the play at work concept a bit further and ask you to consider how playing, period, can impact your attempt to create a team culture. For example, do your teachers have organized opportunities for socialization after the school day ends? Most schools have a social committee that is charged with creating fun events. However, what if the *leadership*—namely those of you reading this book—engendered some opportunities for fun by creating systems for it. For example, as referenced above, many schools are applying SEL principles to adults (CASEL, 2013). Mindfulness, meditation, and yoga are now frequent offerings for teachers after (or during!) school hours. Some schools have had groups of teachers initiate a running club. Games and sports are another way to help your staff to bond. Playing volleyball, bowling, or bingo are great ways to increase connections among staff. Some schools have moved away from such offerings, citing that times are simply too busy and stressful. I would argue that this is more of a reason to offer teachers these types of outlets!

Humor is another powerful force in the workplace. Research has shown that the use of humor by leaders can increase employees' creativity, commitment, job satisfaction, and performance (Evans et al., 2019), though the authors caution that, if used inappropriately, it can lead to employees following suit with inappropriate behavior. Light-hearted and positive humor can increase the level of fun for all staff, and leaders can model this approach and make it acceptable for staff to follow suit (Sterrett, 2015). Unfortunately, it is nearly impossible to explain to you how to make witty comments and be quick with a humorous popular culture reference at a minute's notice. This is an art. *I cannot make you funny*, if you aren't. However, I can help you to visualize a system whereby humor will be a natural outcome, especially when the funny content does not have to come from your own brain. Rather, let the material present itself.

For example, a great system for humor that I inherited from one of my own leadership mentors, longtime Newington (CT) Public Schools middle school principal, David Milardo, is to compile a list of humorous events that had occurred throughout the year. In my version, I would reveal the list to staff at an end-of-year faculty meeting. As this tradition became part of the culture, staff would regularly report humorous events, as they were unfolding. It was common to hear, "Oh, that is going on the list!" This style of tradition—the format is not as important as the *spirit*—helped bring our staff together because humor became a team event. We all looked forward to contributing to the list—even ending up on the list ourselves!, and we most certainly wanted each year's list to be more ridiculous than the one from the year before.

There are a few rules, of course. No one should be part of the festivities without their permission, and, more importantly, this process is not meant to make fun of, demean, or ridicule anyone, whether they are present at the reveal meeting, or not. Further, you can model the light-hearted atmosphere by including many of your own not-so-shiny moments, such as the time you robocalled the entire school community to tell them about an upcoming day off, even though that day off had been moved later in the year by the Board of Education; or the time you wrote an email to your entire staff about communicating with the "public," though you forgot the letter "l;" or the time your mobile phone's automated assistant feature butt-emailed the entire school district while you were dealing with a disciplinary situation. *Good times.*

I would host an optional faculty meeting to reveal the list. This is not a misprint. It says *optional.* Staff would laugh at my presentation, and then I would turn the meeting over to them to share any stories of their own that had not made it onto the official list. I can write a book from those stories, alone! The kindergartener who innocently and enthusiastically yelled out his bus window "Bye, old lady!" to our waving art teacher on bus duty; the time one of our administrative assistants unintentionally locked a teacher in the supply closet at the end of the day; the time a teacher forgot to leave the building and was still inside when the alarm was set. I could go on. The point here is that our work was challenging and draining, and we found a way to bring joy into the work as often as possible. Laughing is a great vehicle for your team's connectedness. Consider how you can create a system where fun and laughter can be regular visitors to your school, even if funny ain't your thing.

## Display Appreciation

Human beings crave affirmation and praise from others. We desire to be appreciated. This fact needs no more explanation than the widespread need for "likes" on social media. Social media outlets such as Facebook, Twitter, and Instagram have quite literally set up mechanisms for other people to formally and publicly announce their appreciation for you wearing that outfit, your cute pet doing something goofy, your kids growing up so darn fast, or, perhaps, your rant about people who put 13 items in their cart and join the "12 items or less" line (or your subsequent rant about why it really should be "12 items or *fewer*"!).

In schools, all educators want to be affirmed for their work as well. Returning to Marzano et al. (2005), another of their 21 Responsibilities of the School Leader is *affirmation*. The authors are clear to point out that this does include recognizing and acknowledging the negative, as well as the positive. However, in terms of building a culture of appreciation, my focus here will be on the positive. Teaching is a difficult profession. To perform at the highest levels requires extreme "locked in" concentration during a lightning-fast school day that is packed with issues that must be addressed in real time. It is an exhausting day. On top of this, most teachers work many hours beyond their contracted time to prepare lessons and examine student work. Teachers are quite justified in wanting their leaders, both formal and otherwise, to notice and appreciate their hard work.

In what ways are staff members appreciated in your building? Ways to show appreciation range from the very formal (i.e. buying lunch for the staff in the faculty lounge, creating Teacher/Nurse/Cafeteria Worker/Bus Driver Appreciation Days, purchasing small gifts for staff birthdays, espousing thanks and gratitude in formal communications, etc.) to the much less formal (i.e. the "You did an amazing job at that parent meeting!" comment when passing in the hallway, the note in the teacher's mailbox about a great lesson, a waived duty to acknowledge a team's extra effort on a project, praising a teacher's work in a meeting with the teacher and a parent, etc.). As long as these efforts are genuine and not undermined by contradictory actions, they will go a long way toward creating an atmosphere of trust and respect. Further, though formal leaders are the drivers and tone setters for the culture of appreciation, teacher leaders can forward this work, considerably, among their peers. When a colleague comes through for you with a resource, helps to divide the labor of organizing an event, or has your back when you are ill by creating substitute plans, let these individuals know how much you appreciate their efforts. Figure 1.3 can help you consider the ways that staff members are appreciated in your building. An editable version of this tool can be found in the eResources collection for this book. What new ways can you envision to appreciate your staff and/or colleagues?

| Present Methods of Appreciation (i.e. buying lunch, organizing a formal event, written appreciation, informal praise, etc.) | Group or Individual Appreciated | Frequency |
|---|---|---|
|  |  |  |
|  |  |  |
|  |  |  |
|  |  |  |
|  |  |  |
| **Proposed Methods of Appreciation** | **Group or Individual Appreciated** | **Frequency** |
|  |  |  |
|  |  |  |
|  |  |  |

*Figure 1.3* Appreciation audit and enhancement tool.

# Build Relationship Equity

In the business world, there is a construct known as "relationship equity." There, the concept is used to consider whether consumers might want to purchase a product or stay loyal to a brand. In psychology, a version of the term applies to the give and take balance in a relationship, such as when a loved one is ill (McPherson et al., 2010). In the work of schools, I will apply this construct to whether individuals want to work with us, or not. Every single interaction we have with stakeholders is an opportunity to either improve or diminish our relationship equity with them. To use an easily relatable economic analogy, if you own a home, you likely pay a mortgage, whereby you make regular payments that increase (at a snail's pace!) the share of the house that is yours. This growing share of the house is your equity. With any relationship, like a home, we hope to acquire and maintain a significant investment in the other person. The quality and quantity of our interactions with others influence the level of relationship equity we build. Each positive interaction builds equity; conversely, each negative interaction diminishes equity. The negative interactions have a more powerful diminishing effect than positive interactions have in building. In other words, one disrespectful comment, one sharp retort, one unprofessional moment, and a whole lot

## What Kind of School Do We Want, Anyway?

of positive interactions can be counteracted in an instant. Those leaders in your school who are masters at building relationship equity are those who look you in the eye when you speak to them. They smile at you often. They read your body language and listen intently to what you are saying in order to provide you what you need. They have excellent interpersonal communication skills, both verbally and nonverbally (Mieliwocki & Fatheree, 2019). These leaders, whether formal or informal, are the ones teachers choose to follow, emulate, and respect. Figure 1.4 shows the conceptual association between relationship equity and actions that enhance and diminish it.

More concretely, think about your own interactions with those you lead, your colleagues, and support personnel. The many individual suggestions for relationship building that precede this discussion can increase relationship equity with others. Consider these questions about your interactions with others in Figure 1.5.

By answering the reflection questions in Figure 1.5 *honestly* (Read: *You are only kidding yourself by lying about your interactions! There is no time like the present to practice the relationship-equity-building skill of honesty!*), you can begin to see your potential to build relationship equity and at what pace. The more positively you answered the questions, the quicker you will build relationship equity, and the less likely you will be to sabotage your efforts with diminishing behaviors, when you have that one, off day.

The importance of building relationship equity may not be readily apparent to you now. *But just wait.* Wait for a problem. Once there is

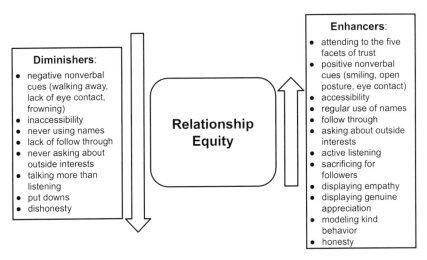

*Figure 1.4* Relationship equity with diminishers and enhancers.

# What Kind of School Do We Want, Anyway?

> 1. Do you use people's names? Every time?
> 2. Do you maintain positive eye contact (short of staring, of course!) when others are speaking to you?
> 3. Does your posture and other body language (i.e. smiling, nodding, open posture, etc.) indicate that you want to be a part of the conversation (as opposed to leaning toward an escape)?
> 4. How often do you follow through on what you say you will do?
> 5. How often do you ask about outside interests of the other person?
> 6. Do you display actively listening (i.e. letting the other person speak first, displaying empathy, paraphrasing, replying with appropriate appreciative noises [i.e. "hmm," "oh," "uh-huh," etc.], asking thoughtful and relevant questions, etc.) to show you are engaged in the conversation and interested in helping the other person?
> 7. Do you avoid using sarcasm or other means to put others down, even if those you would put down are not in your presence?
> 8. How accessible would your teachers/colleagues say you are?
> 9. Would those you lead describe you as "trustworthy" or "kind"?
> 10. Are you regularly honest and transparent with those you lead?

*Figure 1.5* Questions to assess your relationship-equity-building skills in everyday interactions.

adversity, the power of your earned relationship equity will be on display for you, clear as day. If you have worked to build positive relationships as are advocated here, when you send out some incorrect information and then need to retract it, your staff will accept your apology and move on, giving you the benefit of the doubt. Further, if you need that favor, say, a set of volunteers to work on that accreditation committee, positive relationship equity can result in teachers stepping up to help. If you want to collaborate with colleagues on building a new unit of study, they will want to work with you. However, if you are not paying enough attention to building positive relationships, you will lose the trust of your staff and/or colleagues. For example, if you ever show more negative emotion than you should during that difficult faculty meeting, your staff will remember your outburst and fear it will return again. If you criticize a colleague's teaching approach in a flippant manner, good luck getting your colleague to cover your duty when you need to go to that doctor's appointment! Less relationship equity means less trust and engagement, and, as Sinek (2014) and Maslow (1970) reminded us earlier, without that trust, the safety prerequisite of the team is not met. Without engagement, less gets accomplished. Great things will not happen.

## Listening 2.0

In the context of school, listening has another meaning than the micro-level relationship skill that we examined earlier. Namely, consider the work of Marzano et al. (2005) again. Another one of their 21 Responsibilities is the concept of *input*. Here, the authors write about a leader's ability to apply the opinions and ideas of stakeholders to decision making. They caution readers about the dangers of ignoring this important responsibility. Without input from teachers, a leader necessarily removes the team element from the school. The school is *I*, *me*, and *my*, not *we*, *us*, and *ours*. In another foundational, large-scale study of leadership essentials, Kenneth Leithwood and his colleagues included among their main recommendations for leadership impact on student learning that school leaders create "collaborative processes" (Leithwood et al., 2004).

Leaders can effectively provide teachers opportunities for decision making, and Chapter 2 will explore how a coherent system of teams can lead to more participative leadership. However, here, we need to consider the disposition of the leader with respect to input received. For example, in my work with teachers, I often hear from them that their leaders are plenty willing to hear their ideas. However, the input given is often not acted upon. In other words, their ideas are treated as if they are not sound and worthy of implementation. In other cases, teachers have lamented participating as a member of a committee, where they perceive the outcomes to be predetermined, so that their input into the committee work is not meaningful. Ultimately, this lack of meaningful engagement leads to resentment of leaders. The leaders do not respect teachers enough to value their ideas, and the net results could be that teachers stop volunteering for committee work, and/or they might cease making suggestions. The ideas in Chapter 2 about building a system of teams will prove meaningless, if the members of those teams feel disempowered via their leaders rejecting all their ideas. Recall, again, the trust that Finnish society places in its teachers (Sahlberg & Walker, 2021).

This is not to say that leaders need to embrace every idea brought to their attention. Further, it is likely that, for each idea brought forward, there

### What Kind of School Do We Want, Anyway?

is someone in the teaching ranks that is diametrically opposed to it. Thus, even when input is valued and heeded, someone in the school community will view a particular suggestion as a poor idea. Further, individual teachers in their classrooms may not see the big picture perspective that their leaders do. As such, sometimes their ideas are simply not viable, but when decision making is frequently consistent with teacher and colleague input, these teammates will be more receptive to having some ideas rejected due to viability. When leaders ask their teams questions like those shown in Figure 1.6, teachers will begin to feel empowered and part of a team.

Figure 1.6 consists of possible inquiries that illustrate that leaders value others' contributions. Of course, none of this is helpful without the follow through discussed earlier. If leaders hear ideas and then act upon other ideas or, worse yet, only their own original thoughts, then the message delivered is: *I'm a phony who is only asking for your ideas to seem like I am listening. I'm really not!* The more you actually listen to the input of teachers and

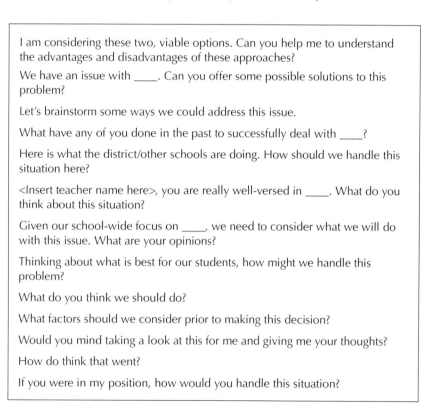

*Figure 1.6* Participative leadership inquiries.

colleagues, the more you will be seen as "real" and accessible. Teachers will perceive that they truly have a voice (DeWitt, 2017). Trust will follow (Fullan & Kirtman, 2019; Sterrett, 2015). The message delivered is, *I really do need and want your input and help!*

Be sure to orient your teams as problem-solving entities, as opposed to simply forums to raise issues. Some leaders, attempting be the "hero" and handle all problems, big and small, miss that their teams exist to help them solve problems of practice. In overlooking this key truth, they are content to solicit problems from staff members that they, the leaders, must then solve. These inquiries resemble:

What concerns do you have for me?

Does anyone have an issue to raise?

These are innocent-enough questions, and there is nothing inherently wrong with them, so long as the staff members raising the issues are also expected to help craft solutions. I frame this difference as teaching all members of the school community to be problem solvers, as opposed to problem identifiers. If leadership allows staff to help solve problems by valuing their input, staff are empowered (Fullan & Kirtman, 2019). It goes without saying that this approach improves collegiality, as the team works toward solutions, not just formal leaders. Further, all staff members become more comfortable taking risks to make suggestions. A frame of reference for the problem solver/identifier dichotomy can be found in Figure 1.7. This tool can be

| Are you a . . . | |
|---|---|
| **Problem Identifier?** | **Problem Solver?** |
| I focus on and point out the flaws in others' ideas. | I notice and focus on the value in others' ideas. |
| I offer criticism with no solutions. | I point out challenges with possible solutions. |
| I say, "We already did that, and it didn't work." | I say, "Maybe this time, it will work because we could try . . . " |
| I have a fixed mindset. | I have a growth mindset. |
| I wait for others to solve problems. | I own and solve problems. |
| I give up easily. | I persevere. |
| I see problems as "yours" to solve. | I see problems as "ours" to solve. |

*Figure 1.7* Problem solver versus problem identifier tool.

used for individuals to self-assess their own tendencies, with an eye toward improvement that will produce more problem solvers on your team. I find that few educators would ever admit to the behaviors on the left side of the graphic (problem identifier characteristics). However, staff members are certainly quick to recognize these behaviors in their colleagues! By visualizing these less-desirable behaviors in particularly difficult colleagues, well-meaning teachers looking to capitalize on our three guiding principles will use knowledge of these "nonexample" colleagues as a template for what not to do and, therefore, will improve their own tendencies and practice.

## Messaging

Marzano et al. (2005) included among their 21 Responsibilities of the School Leader being an *optimizer*. In this responsibility, the authors wrote about how leaders should be a positive presence and voice, communicating consistently that the team can overcome obstacles and address challenges successfully. To illustrate this concept for teachers, I often provide them the extreme negative case as a counterpoint. Consider this faculty meeting message:

> Well, everyone, we really underachieved in the last round of state testing. Our students are increasingly needy and less skilled. Our parents are less helpful than in the past. Our community sees us as a failure, and I can't really disagree. We just aren't very effective. But ... go get 'em!

It is difficult to imagine any teachers being inspired to put in extra effort to achieve better results after that hopeless soliloquy. Conversely, leaders, in all roles, need to communicate a positive, team approach that can inspire and motivate. Consider this improved message:

> Team, our scores last year were not where any of us wanted them to be, and we are facing many significant challenges. However, we have revamped some aspects of our curricula to make them more relevant and impactful, and we have implemented new systems for social and emotional learning and intervention for students not performing at grade level. We will teach them better in Tier I, and then we will accelerate them more effectively in Tiers II and III. I want you to remember when we faced the challenge of our less-than-desirable parent survey results. With our attention to communication, our scores improved dramatically. We can do this!

Who wouldn't want to work in the second environment, when compared to the hopeless first one?

Ultimately, the intention of leaders' communication matters less than the perception of those receiving the messages (Musgrave, 2018). Thus, messages of trust to build the perception of psychological safety discussed earlier in the chapter will help move teachers toward increased commitment and favorable team results. In addition, emotional state and delivery are critical to receptivity by an audience. David Musgrave, a consultant who applies brain research to workplace safety, put it best when he stated, "Calm, centered and engaged is appropriate, rather than frustrated, fatigued, stressed or distracted" (2018, p. 50). Teachers want to know that their leaders believe in them and have a handle on the work of leading the school, connecting back to the competence facet of trust (Tschannen-Moran & Gareis, 2015). Further, they do not want to work under or with those who are prone to losing their cool over the work.

The impacts of your messages are determined in part by these key factors: rhetorical force, retrievability, and resonance (Berezin & Lamont, 2016). The authors, in examining public health policy messages, explained that rhetorical force includes the techniques the leader uses to make the message something memorable and powerful. In a school context, tapping into people's emotions, such as through displaying data for a subgroup of students who are not seeing success, can be a means to motivate others to change (Fullan, 2007). Retrievability refers to how readily those hearing a message can access the message later. Consider repetition and branding here. As a principal, the consistent message I always repeated was about staff members viewing themselves as leaders and comporting themselves as such. Finally, resonance involves how closely your message aligns with others' beliefs and allows them to connect to your ideas. Here, I implore you to find the common ground as a starting point. For example, reminding teachers that you all want what is best for your students is a foundation with which few educators could ever argue. The same goes for the general statement that all students can learn. On top of these truths with near-ubiquitous agreement, messages with less widespread appeal can be layered. In short, messaging substance and style matter. In your efforts to lead, consider what are the most important messages for your school or team and make sure these messages are ones staff hear and see regularly and consistently. We will examine this topic a bit more in Chapter 2, when we consider how your system of teams benefits from your messaging about teams' purposes and their connections to the big picture.

 ## Pulling It All Together

Anecdotally, I recall an administrator whom the faculty did not respect. The reasons were not due to what the administrator did not do well—conversely, the administrator was actually widely seen as extremely intelligent and capable with the mechanical aspects of leadership (i.e. creating schedules, designing systems, completing requirements of teacher evaluation, etc.). Rather, the leader was roundly and consistently criticized by the teaching staff for not building relationships with them. An example cited by many in the school was that this principal would often pick up a piece of paper off the floor to keep the school looking orderly, rather than greet a teacher the leader was passing in the hallway. This leader would sometimes appear deep in thought when walking through the halls and, thus, not acknowledge a teacher just a few feet away. This principal was creating a culture of transactional compliance, not a transformational culture that fulfills the ideals of empowerment, collegiality, and risk taking.

In support of the preceding discussion about building relationships to foster the three foundational principles, leaders, both formal and informal, must model the relationship behaviors desired in those they lead. Humility and gratitude should be the norm. The leader who pretends to know it all (This must be a facade because educational leadership is simply too complex and dynamic for anyone to have all the answers. Thus, if you are the "Know-It-All" leader, then you are a lying liar who lies! *Pants on fire*, and all!) does nothing more than lose respect from staff. Showing that you do not know everything and that you can learn from those you lead is a show of strength, not weakness. For example, I was a teacher (Earth science and American history, to be exact) and assistant principal at the middle school level. However, after several years in those roles, I was promoted to the principalship of an elementary school. At the time of my appointment, I knew about solid, effective pedagogy and working with families and young people, but I did not know the first thing about teaching kids how to read or recess or kids crying at school or preschool or kids wanting to hug you. It was a whole new world for me. I spent much time with teachers in the new building, just observing their work and conversing with them about what they were doing. It was humbling, indeed. Rather than tell the staff that I knew more about their job than they did, I told them I was going to learn from them. Once I was caught up to speed, then we, together, could learn how to get even better.

A fitting place to end this chapter of foundations, is how to handle situations when you are wrong, or, at least, when it appears that you have been wrong. In a very interesting study from the world of commerce, an apology has been shown to be twice as effective at changing unhappy customers' negative reviews than offering them monetary compensation (Abeler et al., 2010). From an economic perspective, this can be translated to: *Apologies save us money!* However, in our highly interpersonal world of education, the apology is not a bottom-line changer. Rather, it works to build relationship equity, and it shows leaders to be real, genuine people. Concretely, apologies can rebuild trust (Martin, 2010), which, as was outlined earlier in the chapter, is the key to building a strong team. By admitting fault, you are showing your staff and colleagues that you care enough about them to be honest, which supports one of the facets of trust (Tschannen-Moran & Gareis, 2015). Further, you can display empathy through your articulation of how your mistakes might have affected others. I am sorry to say (*See what I did there?*) that apologies, when warranted, can contribute to the trusting culture needed to move schools forward.

## Summary

This chapter presented three foundational principles to promote teacher leadership. The principles are:

(a) **empowerment**: Our staff members feel competent and believe that they are equipped to make decisions in the best interest of our students and school. Our teachers have sound ideas that can improve what we do;

(b) **collegiality**: Our staff works together to solve problems of practice. We do not work in isolation. What we learn, we share; and,

(c) **risk taking**: We do not advance if we do not try new things and experiment. We are not afraid to do things differently.

The foundation of a strong team culture in your school is built through relationships among all adults within the system. At the most basic level, team members need to feel that their safety needs are met. Individuals' natural reactions to safety are to trust and cooperate and work to help leadership meet its vision. In order to engender trust, leaders sacrifice for those they lead, as well as attend to the five facets of trust: vulnerability, benevolence, honesty, openness, and competence.

This chapter outlined concrete ways to build and maintain positive professional relationships. Small moments, when leaders can be helpful to those they lead and follow through on requests and promises, are impactful. Active listening; displaying empathy; supervising with a growth focus; learning and using stakeholders' names; providing opportunities for staff fun; displaying genuine appreciation for effort; engendering trust; and providing positive, team-oriented messages are concrete strategies to improve relationships and build relationship equity.

Valuing teachers' input is important to building a team mentality, as is providing the expectation that teachers will contribute to solutions as problem solvers. Modeling humility and gratitude for staff, as well as apologizing for mistakes, can build trust in leadership by displaying your honesty and empathy and, in turn, improve the team climate.

## Questions to Consider for Chapter 1:
### *So, What Kind of a School Do We Want, Anyway?*

1. Think about the three foundational principles (empowerment, collegiality, and risk taking). Consider your responses to the *Would Teachers Rather?* screening tool in Figure 1.2. How established do you think these ideals are in your school?
2. Who are the individuals in your school that you can count on to be the positive leadership core of the school? Why did you select these individuals?
3. Is your school professionally safe for staff members? If not, what is holding them back from experiencing the feeling of professional safety?
4. Of the relationship equity enhancers, which do you witness most often? Least often? In what concrete ways can you, personally, model more relationship equity enhancing behavior?

5. Consider the five facets of trust: vulnerability, benevolence, honesty, openness, and competence. What would those you lead or work with say about your behaviors within each of these facets?
6. Do formal leaders in your school value teachers' input through their actions? If so, how? If not, in what ways can value for teachers' input be improved?

# References

Abeler, J., Calaki, J., Andree, K., & Basek, C. (2010). The power of apology. *Economics Letters, 107*, 233–235. https://doi.org/10.1016/j.econlet.2010.01.033

Berezin, M., & Lamont, M. (2016). Mutuality, mobilization, and messaging for health promotion: Toward collective cultural change. *Social Science and Medicine, 165*, 201–205. https://doi.org/10.1016/j.socscimed.2016.07.040

Berg, J. H. (2019). Make time for play. *Educational Leadership, 76*(4), 87–88.

Collaborative for Academic Social and Emotional Learning. (2013). *Effective social and emotional learning programs.* https://doi.org/http://casel.org/wp-content/uploads/2016/01/2013-casel-guide-1.pdf

Covey, S. R. (2004). *The 7 habits of highly effective people: Powerful lessons in personal change* (Rev. ed.). Simon & Schuster.

DeWitt, P. M. (2017). *Collaborative leadership: 6 influences that matter most.* Corwin Press.

Donaldson, M. L. (2016). Teacher evaluation reform: Focus, feedback, and fear. *Educational Leadership, 73*(8), 72–76.

Drago-Severson, E., & Blum-DeStefano, J. (2018). *Leading change together: Developing educator capacity within schools and systems.* ASCD.

Epitropoulos, A. (2019). 10 signs of a toxic school culture. *Education Update, 61*(9), 4.

Evans, J. B., Slaughter, J. E., Ellis, A. P. J., & Rivin, J. M. (2019). Gender and the evaluation of humor at work. *Journal of Applied Psychology, 104*, 1077–1087. https://doi.org/10.1037/apl0000395

Fullan, M. (2007). *The NEW meaning of educational change* (4th ed.). Teachers College Press.

Fullan, M., & Kirtman, L. (2019). *Coherent school leadership: Forging clarity from complexity.* ASCD.

Hargreaves, A., & Fullan, M. (2012). *Professional capital: Transforming teaching in every school.* Teachers College Press.

Hargreaves, A., & Fullan, M. (2013). The power of professional capital: With an investment in collaboration, teachers become nation builders. *Journal of Staff Development, 34*(3), 36–39.

Howard, P., Becker, C., Wiebe, S., Carter, M., Gouzouasis, P., Mclarnon, M., Richardson, P., Ricketts, K., & Schuman, L. (2018). Creativity and pedagogical innovation: Exploring teachers' experiences of risk-taking. *Journal of Curriculum Studies, 50,* 850–864. https://doi.org/10.1080/00220272.2018.1479451

Leana, C. R. (2011). The missing link in school reform. *Stanford Social Innovation Review, 9*(4), 30–35.

Leithwood, K., Louis, K. S., Anderson, S., & Wahlstrom, K. (2004). *Review of research: How leadership influences student learning.* The Wallace Foundation. https://doi.org/10.1007/978-90-481-2660-6

Liu, Y., Visone, J., Mongillo, M. B., & Lisi, P. (2019). What matters to teachers if evaluation is meant to help them improve? *Studies in Educational Evaluation, 61,* 41–54. https://doi.org/10.1016/j.stueduc.2019.01.006

Martin, A. M. (2010). Owning up and lowering down: The power of apology. *The Journal of Philosophy, 107,* 534–553. https://www.jstor.org/stable/pdf/29778053.pdf?refreqid=excelsior%3A7a85cde2c2045d81f0c30faebac0b31e

Marzano, R. J., Waters, T., & McNulty, B. A. (2005). *School leadership that works: From research to results.* ASCD.

Maslow, A. (1970). *Motivation and personality* (3rd ed.). Longman.

McPherson, C. J., Wilson, K. G., Leclerc, C., & Chyurlia, L. (2010). The balance of give and take in caregiver-partner relationships: An examination of self-perceived burden, relationship equity, and quality of life from the perspective of care recipients following stroke. *Rehabilitation Psychology, 55*(2), 194–203. https://doi.org/10.1037/a0019359

Mieliwocki, R., & Fatheree, J. (2019). *Adventures in teacher leadership: Pathways, strategies, and inspiration for every teacher.* ASCD.

Musgrave, D. (2018). Brain-aligned leadership messaging. *Professional Safety, 63*(11), 50–51.

Novick, B. (2015). 10 tips for tackling difficult conversations. *Educational Leadership, 72*, 80–81.

Posey, A. (2019). *Engage the brain: How to design for learning that taps into the power of emotion.* ASCD.

Sahlberg, P., & Walker, T. D. (2021). *In teachers we trust: The Finnish way to world-class schools.* W. W. Norton & Company.

Sinek, S. (2014). *Why good leaders make you feel safe* [TED talk]. https://www.youtube.com/watch?v=lmyZMtPVodo

Sterrett, W. (2015). *Igniting teacher leadership: How do I empower my teachers to lead and learn?* ASCD.

Stone, D., Patton, B., & Heen, S. (2010). *Difficult conversations: How to discuss what matters most.* Penguin Books.

Treasure, J. (2011). *5 ways to listen better* [TED talk]. https://www.ted.com/talks/julian_treasure_5_ways_to_listen_better?language=en#t-375135

Tschannen-Moran, M., & Gareis, C. (2015). Principals, trust, and cultivating vibrant schools. *Societies, 5*(2), 256–276. https://doi.org/10.3390/soc5020256

Visone, J. D. (2018). Developing social and decisional capital in US National Blue Ribbon Schools. *Improving Schools, 21*(2), 158–172. https://doi.org/10.1177/1365480218755171

# How Can Our Systems Support the Three Foundational Principles?

"Why did we even have to go to that meeting? It was a complete waste of time!" grumbled Jean to her colleague, Steve, as she left her Merryport Middle School Improvement Committee meeting. During the Tuesday afternoon meeting, the committee had examined some recent fall benchmark assessment data, with an emphasis on what the data meant for what students know and are able to do. Unfortunately, some of the data were not yet entered into the data warehousing system, so the dataset did not include all classes' results, and, thus, no concrete conclusions could be drawn by the committee. Without enough to discuss with the dataset, the conversation shifted to the intervention process in the school, which many teachers viewed as ineffective and frustrating.

One day earlier, on Monday, the school's Professional Learning Committee had met to discuss teachers' learning needs. The conversation was led by the school's reading and language arts consultant and a Grade 7 math teacher, who are the co-chairs of the committee. However, the committee had no overlapping membership with the School Improvement Committee, and, since their meeting was prior to the aforementioned Improvement Committee meeting, the Professional Learning Committee did not ground their discussion in student data, which, as you already know, were not all available, anyway. Rather, the conversation followed teachers' wants and suggestions. The co-chairs made a list of suggestions that they planned to email to the school's principal, Angela. Angela routinely asked for this type of input. However, as Chuck, a member of the Professional Learning Committee, stated at the end of the meeting, "It really doesn't matter what goes on our list. Angela has her own plan for our workshops this year, anyway." Several nods in the group affirmed Chuck's pessimistic view of the value of the committee's input. As with the School Improvement

Committee, members questioned their purpose. "I am basically here to serve my time and have something positive to write in my professionalism section of our teacher evaluation system," bluntly stated Ellen, a Grade 8 science teacher.

On Wednesday of the next week, Monica, a Grade 6 language arts teacher, had some concerns about a student of hers. She initiated a conversation in the hallway with the reading and language arts consultant, Carmen, who tried to advise her.

"I am not sure what to do with Freddy," stated Monica.

"At the School Improvement Committee meeting last week, we discussed making some changes to our intervention systems. I think some of what we discussed will be helpful to you," Carmen answered.

"Well, that is sure good to hear. But, how would I have known about this, if we hadn't run into one another? I always wonder what goes on in those meetings, behind closed doors."

"It is all in our school improvement plan, usually."

"What school improvement plan? I have never seen that!" reacted Monica.

The next day, on Thursday, Angela conducted a faculty meeting after school. During the faculty meeting, she introduced some business items related to new lockdown drill procedures and a social and emotional learning initiative, which each took 10 more minutes than she had planned. The time overrun left her with only 15 minutes remaining to devote to the professional learning topic of the afternoon—raising the rigor level of questioning. Jean turned to Chuck and whispered, "Why do we need to learn this? My questioning is just fine. Where did this come from?" Chuck nodded his agreement.

Merryport Middle School exhibits some positive practices: non-administrative staff members co-chair an important committee about professional learning; its principal solicits input from teachers; staff members care about student success; worthy changes to practices are being recommended, etc. However, the scenario also highlights shortcomings that are all too common in many schools.

Systems are not ideally operational at this middle school. Coherence is lacking. Jean and Chuck participated in meetings for which they could not articulate a purpose. Monica wanted to help her student, but, except for a happenstance, teacher-initiated conversation with her Reading and Language

How Can Systems Support the Principles?

| | |
|---|---|
| **empowerment** | Our staff members feel competent and believe that they are equipped to make decisions in the best interest of our students and school. Our teachers have sound ideas that can improve what we do. |
| **collegiality** | Our staff works together to solve problems of practice. We do not work in isolation. What we learn, we share. |
| **risk taking** | We do not advance if we do not try new things and experiment. We are not afraid to do things differently. |

*Figure 2.1* The three foundational principles to empower teacher leadership.

Arts Consultant, she would not have known that changes were coming to the school's intervention system. Chuck noted that Angela solicits teacher input regularly, but she does not value what the teachers have shared when she makes decisions. Finally, Angela rushed to present professional learning that her teachers could not connect to their vision of what needed to be improved. Returning to the three foundational principles of *empowerment, collegiality,* and *risk taking,* which are outlined in Figure 2.1, the teachers at Merryport Middle School are not empowered to fully participate in the leadership of the school. Collegiality may be present in pockets and superficially through the committee work, but we are left to wonder about the level of investment of teachers on committees, if they believe their time is being wasted. Finally, risk taking is stifled when teachers believe that their ideas are not valued.

In this chapter, you will consider a systems approach to ensuring these three principles come alive in your school. In other words, Chapter 1 helped you to consider the relationship foundations that are required to support the three principles, but, now, what leadership decisions and structures can move your school toward operationalizing these ideals? In yet other words, how can you set up your school, logistically, to support empowerment, collegiality, and risk taking? While you ponder these questions, let's examine systems and the construct of systems thinking.

## A Bit about Systems

In my first career, as an outpatient physical therapist, my daily work was often devoted to helping patients regain function through healing muscles, tendons, ligaments, joints, and bones. Together, these types of tissues work together as a team—the musculoskeletal system. Patients are referred to therapy because one or more elements of this system are not working properly, causing the system to function below optimal capacity. For example, for a patient whose neck is injured due to whiplash suffered in a car accident, the neck muscles might be locked in a protective state of spasm, preventing the patient from moving her head. To help the patient regain proper function, it might seem logical to treat the spasming muscles. However, this assumption might be incomplete. To treat the proper element of the system, it is important to accurately diagnose the root cause of the dysfunction. If the muscles were locked up, not because they themselves were injured, but because they were protecting a bulging intervertebral disc, then simply relaxing the muscles will not bring the system back to working order. To treat systems is to learn the root of the problem, and then address that cause, not the resulting symptoms.

For other patients in my clinic, multiple systems were involved. For example, patients with Parkinson's disease do not have difficulty with simple movements because their muscles are faulty, though their symptoms manifest as musculoskeletal. Tremors and difficulty with voluntary motion are not the result of muscles that cannot contract properly; rather, the signals the muscles have received from another system—the nervous system—are to blame. Thus, the treatment plan involves influencing the brain to improve patients' function. In this case, there is a cause and effect scenario. *If I influence this situation here, it will affect this other situation over there.* In systems thinking, actions that affect one element often have far-reaching consequences on other elements within the system.

Before we can apply the concept of systems to the complex work of schools, we should take some time to consider systems themselves. Systems expert Donella Meadows, in her influential, posthumous work *Thinking in Systems: A Primer* (2008), described a system as a set of things that, when organized together, produce a pattern of behavior and accomplish something. Systems are, for organizations such as businesses, hospitals, governments, and schools, the way things get done. The "how" of a system includes such abstract elements as the flow of information, decision points, and the system's overall purpose or function. Flow of information includes communication channels in a people-oriented organization, like a school. Who shares what with whom (i.e. top-down, laterally, two-way, etc.)? When does sharing happen (i.e. regularly, as needed, rarely, etc.)? How does the sharing happen (i.e. verbally, electronically, by chance, etc.)? Decision points might answer a question about who has the authority to determine an outcome. Is it an individual, or is it a team of people? The purpose of the organization (i.e. profit, service, student achievement, etc.) will likely drive a pattern of behavior within the system.

The pattern of behavior in a system adapts to, or outright resists, pressures from outside the system. Anyone who has ever tried to lead any meaningful change in a school knows exactly how powerful that resistance can be! Further, the complex interactions of elements of the system mean that changes to systems are not only difficult to come by, but they are also complex and go beyond the linear thinking of cause and effect (Meadows, 2008; Stroh, 2015). Thus, systems can often best be represented pictorially, as the linear and sequential nature of the written word do not "do justice" to the simultaneous interactions of different aspects of the system.

When leaders leverage knowledge about systems to problem solve and improve an organization's function through strategic decision making, this is called *systems thinking*. In an informative text, *Systems Thinking for Social Change: A Practical Guide to Solving Complex Problems, Avoiding Unintended Consequences, and Achieving Lasting Results*, David Peter Stroh (2015) explained that systems thinking is more complex than conventional thinking about problem solving. This is because leaders who are systems thinkers must consider the whole system—the proverbial "big picture," including the system's many elements' interactions and interrelationships; concurrent happenings; and, in the case of organizations, people who are influencing and being affected by actions.

To help illustrate what it means to consider the entire system, Stroh created binary comparisons to contrast systems thinking and conventional thinking. For example, in conventional thinking, solutions to problems can be obvious and not difficult to find, whereby systems thinking involves solutions to problems that are not obvious and are often very challenging to determine. Conventional thinking can include policy changes that will meet with both short-term and long-term success; however, systems solutions are long-term and do not typically result from short-term fixes, which often make matters worse. Conventional thinking involves making the individual system elements better, while systems thinking looks to improve the relationship among the elements of the system. Finally, whereby conventional thinkers will successfully attack many independent improvements at the same time, system thinkers must prioritize, strategize, and skillfully implement a few coordinated changes over the long-term to meet with success. In this text, you will find systems thinking principles embedded throughout the consistent application of the three foundational principles.

Stroh continued to outline a systems thinking response to the four challenges of change, which he identified as motivation, collaboration, focus, and learning. Using a systems approach can motivate those in an organization to change for a variety of reasons, including that people come to understand their own role in the overall system functioning, even their contributions to obtaining undesirable results. Further, this understanding of role can help foster collaboration to forge a better path and achieve different results. With an understanding of the larger system, conceptualized as "perspective taking" by other authors (Drago-Severson & Blum-DeStefano, 2018, p. 7), actors within the system can strategically adopt only a select few high-leverage interventions. Finally, by recognizing that we might be contributing to the system in less-than-optimal ways, members can accept that continuous learning is needed to achieve better.

Systems thinking is intricately connected with this book. In Chapter 1, I emphasized motivation through culture building. In this chapter, a focus is defining roles and purposes, to help individual teachers see their connection to the overall operation. Also, continual learning is a focus of Chapter 3, where you will examine how to use the most readily available resource at teachers' disposal—*each other*—to propel learning and growth to new heights.

Like the human body, a school is a complex amalgam of many dynamic elements that, hopefully, work cooperatively to positively influence student outcomes and create a healthy school culture. As we now know, systems involve elements that affect each other (Meadows, 2008; Stroh, 2015). When an element of a system is not working properly, the rest of that system can be affected, and the outputs can be subpar. For example, how often do transportation limitations (i.e. busing, start times, etc.) impact decisions at the school level? How often do politics at the level of the board of education result in revised programming at the school level? These two examples are largely out of the control of school and teacher leaders. Conversely, how often does the schedule in your building place limitations on programming? How often do communication breakdowns impact what happens in the school and how teachers feel about what they are asked to do? How often do lack of teacher buy-in and/or understanding of initiatives negatively affect success? These latter three questions involve constructs that are influenced, to a large degree, by the school's leadership—scheduling and communication. Thus, school leaders can have great influence—for better or worse!—on systems in their buildings.

*I love it when we cannot run a quality program for students because it won't work in the schedule, and I also appreciate it when I am left out of the loop about decisions made that affect me ... said no teacher, ever!* I always tell aspiring school leaders that leaders are builders of systems. The most effective systems do not create themselves, under most circumstances. And these systems greatly impact the quality of work and learning in your school. This chapter will help you strategically create systems to enhance the three foundations principles.

## Systems Thinking in Schools

Hall and Hord (2019) asserted that leadership-led change in schools often fails due to leaders ignoring relevant parts of a system, while only attending to other parts. An incomplete understanding of all the components of a functioning system can lead to inadequate solutions. Effective leaders pay attention to all parts of systems.

Within a school, systems help to answer many questions about how work will get done. They might influence how a teacher handles a disciplinary situation, requests intervention for a student, or obtains information about upcoming school events. Systems help staff members make decisions more easily, as they impose an order to their work and provide predictability to procedures, protocols, participation structures, forums, and communication channels.

In their widely respected guidebook for data-driven decision making, *Data Wise: A Step-by-Step Guide to Using Assessment Results to Improve Teaching and Learning* (Boudett et al., 2013; Boudett & Moody, 2013), editors Kathryn Boudett, Elizabeth City, and Richard Murnane outlined how to create a system for using data effectively in school improvement planning. Their recommendations had three aspects: adopting a school improvement process, creating a system of teams, and allocating time for teacher collaboration. In terms of a school improvement process, effectiveness involves more than just creating a document, the school improvement plan. Questions to be answered here include: Who will write the plan? What data will be used to craft the plan? What will the timeline be? How will teachers come to know the plan and understand their individual and collective responsibilities within the plan? How and when will the success of the plan be evaluated?

To create a system of teams for data-driven decision making, the editors and contributors suggested identifying which groups will be tasked with what aspects of the data work and prescribing the flow of information among teams. These teams would include the instructional data teams, which are organized by grade level (at the elementary level, typically) or department (at the secondary level, typically), and a school-wide data team. Representation from the instructional data teams on the school-wide data team helps to ensure continuity of the work across teams. They also recommend a district-wide data team to complete a three-tiered system for data-driven analysis and planning.

Finally, in order to provide for the collaboration needed to effectively perform data-driven decision-making work, teachers need to be scheduled in such a way that they can physically meet regularly. These three general recommendations will be important as this chapter continues.

There are more systems functioning in a school than can be adequately addressed in this chapter or, even, book. Thus, I will focus on systems that support our three guiding principles of empowerment, collegiality, and risk taking. As a strategic leader or leadership team, you can design systems within your school to move toward these ideals. First, we will consider what these systems can do for your school logistically. One way to examine the complex construct of systems thinking is to consider questions that this approach can address. A list of questions that a systems-thinking approach can potentially help answer is found in Figure 2.2.

With these questions in mind, we will focus upon how leadership decision making with respect to systems can empower staff and encourage collaboration and risk taking. Our brief treatment of systems and systems thinking is included to help frame the solutions suggested in this chapter. Specifically, this chapter will examine ways your scheduling, teams, communication, and school improvement planning can all support the three foundational principles, while leveraging systems thinking.

## Schedule Considerations for Functioning Systems

Scheduling is a complex challenge that includes many factors: part-time teachers' availabilities, intervention needs, student offerings, number of teachers, curricular offerings, contracts for teachers and other bargaining units (i.e. cafeteria staff, bus drivers, etc.), stakeholder input, etc. Scheduling also has far-reaching effects on a school's functioning. For the purpose of

How Can Systems Support the Principles?

> How does information flow from a meeting to the wider staff?
> 
> What are the connections among different teams and committees within the school, and how do these pieces fit together?
> 
> How does this process work here at our school?
> 
> What is the chain of command for this issue?
> 
> What forum exists for this conversation?
> 
> If this happens, how will it affect other things?
> 
> Who is involved in making which decisions?
> 
> Who initiates this process?
> 
> What is the timeline for this to happen?
> 
> How can we work more efficiently?
> 
> What are different individuals' roles in that situation?
> 
> What is the purpose of this action/team/committee?
> 
> What is the root cause of this situation?
> 
> What strategic action can address this particular problem?
> 
> How does this situation look from different vantage points within the school?

*Figure 2.2* Systems thinking questions for schools.

our discussion, scheduling can impact collegiality in a very concrete way. Namely, as stated above, if leadership espouses that teachers should be working together in professional learning communities (PLCs) and using data to drive instruction, then they need to be available at the same time. Thus, common planning time should be a very early consideration in the creation of any schedule (Boudett & Moody, 2013). The actual mechanism for accomplishing this is so contextually dependent that any generic treatment is watered down to essentially: *Schedule the teachers who need to attend PLCs as free at the same time at least once a week so they can meet.* For those who prefer the visual approach, consider the simplistic schedule example in Figure 2.3. In the schedule shown for one sample day, a team's worth of teachers, say a grade level of elementary teachers or a departmental group of secondary teachers, are all free for one of their planning blocks during that day. Thus, the team's PLC meeting could occur then. Obviously, for common planning time to be prioritized, leaders need to situate it on the grid *first*, filling in teaching and other responsibilities afterward. This approach works

How Can Systems Support the Principles?

| Period | 1 | 2 | 3 | 4 | 5 | 6 | 7 | 8 |
|---|---|---|---|---|---|---|---|---|
| Teacher A | Class | Class | Plan | Class | Lunch | Plan | Class | Class |
| Teacher B | Class | Class | Plan | Lunch | Class | Class | Class | Plan |
| Teacher C | Class | Class | Plan | Plan | Lunch | Class | Class | Class |
| Teacher D | Plan | Class | Plan | Lunch | Class | Class | Class | Class |

*Figure 2.3* Generic schedule with common planning time for four teachers for one school day.

so long as there are at least as many places for students to go during the common planning block (i.e. study halls or other classes) as there are teachers who need the time available. Again, this is contextually dependent. Of course, simply putting teachers into the same room at the same time and telling them to collaborate will not necessarily engender collegial work, but it is a prerequisite for effective collaboration. To engender productive teamwork, we will examine norms, processes, and roles later in this chapter.

With team members physically in place, another critical scheduling consideration for teams is when to strategically schedule their meetings. Though the team system will be discussed in a later section, as far as scheduling is concerned, the timing of teams' meetings should be considered when an annual schedule is created, typically over the summer months or as a new school year begins. Though there will be many unknowns that arise throughout the course of the school year, some important considerations can be anticipated. For example, consider the timing of your School-Wide Data Team's meetings. This team, as will be discussed later in this chapter, will be charged with examining school-wide data sets. As such, to schedule this team's meetings, leaders should first consult the district or school assessment calendar so that the data team meetings can be scheduled shortly after the availability of assessment data. Note that the day after major benchmark assessments are completed is not ideal. First, some students are, inevitably, absent during the assessments, and make-up tests are required. Second, you will surely draw the rightful ire of whoever you charge with compiling data sets with a day or less for turnaround! Generally speaking, anywhere from a week to two weeks after an assessment window closes is a logical time to pencil in a School-Wide Data Team meeting.

In this same example, another consideration for this particular team's meeting date is the schedule of the District-Wide Data Team (if one exists). If a district team will provide information from which the school-based team might benefit, then scheduling the school-based team a few days to a week after the district team might be logical. The preceding examples are some basic schedule considerations to support our three foundational principles, since true collaboration begins with teachers being available at the same time and being provided needed information to perform their work. Next, we will more formally consider a system of teams that supports the three foundational principles.

## A System of Empowering, Collaborative Teams

Another strategic way to empower and encourage collegiality is to create a system of teams to manage the work of the school. For those reading this book who are not formal leaders, know that leadership work in a school is so voluminous and complex that no one individual or even small team of formal school leaders can be effective without the help of many others (Leithwood et al., 2004). This construct of sharing the leadership workload and responsibility is known as *distributed leadership* (Diamond & Spillane, 2016; Spillane, 2006; Spillane et al., 2001). If you are strategic in creating a system of teams, the work becomes much more manageable, and teachers are empowered to contribute to the decision-making process, which necessarily requires collegiality, and, by the way, leads to better results (Fullan & Kirtman, 2019).

The first question you might ask is: *What teams do we need?* Figure 2.4 is a list of some of the key teams a school might consider. This is not an exhaustive listing, but this is a solid set of teams to tackle many of the most important elements of a school's work. Your school likely has some of these teams in place already, though the teams might have different names than presented here. Focus more on the team's purpose than the name. Note, also, that some of these recommended teams could be multiple roles for a single team in your school, or these teams might overlap roles. For example, the proposed work of the School-Wide Data Team could be fully operationalized within the Leadership Team in some schools.

Team membership should, as often as possible, be representative of your school's stakeholders, being strategic when needed. For example, each of the teams should have representation from across grade levels and/or departments, though some teams (i.e. crisis and climate teams) will likely be heavily represented with non-classroom staff members, such as nurses,

## How Can Systems Support the Principles?

| Team | Purpose |
|---|---|
| Leadership Team | advises the formal leaders; solves problems; sets direction; provides for participative decision making and distributed leadership |
| School-Wide Data Team | examines school-level data; creates and monitors school improvement plan; communicates to staff about school improvement plan progress; directs work of instructional data teams (i.e. grade or department) |
| Instructional Leadership Team | oversees professional learning; discusses curriculum, instruction, and assessment; oversees school improvement academic action plan(s) |
| Equity Team | discusses matters related to equity; provides leadership for staff discussions of systemic inequalities; advocates for equitable experiences for all students; assists in recruiting a diverse staff |
| Security Team | creates and monitors school safety plan; monitors safety drills; advises formal leaders about safety concerns |
| Crisis Team | responds to crises within the school; evaluates and adjusts crisis response protocols; educates staff about their role in crisis situations |
| School Climate Team | examines behavioral and attendance data; oversees school improvement climate action plan (i.e. positive behavioral interventions and supports, restorative practices, social and emotional learning, etc.) |
| Student Intervention Team | serves as part of the school's tiered intervention system; provides a forum to discuss student needs within academic, behavioral, and social/emotional areas; advises teachers and monitors progress |
| (Student) Parent Teacher Organization | engages parents in the work of the school; helps implement school improvement parent engagement action plan(s) |

*Figure 2.4* Key teams to support empowerment, collegiality, and risk taking.

psychologists, social workers, special education case managers, paraprofessionals, etc. Some of the empowerment from a system of teams derives from their representative nature. By having teams assist with decision making, decisions can be viewed as representing voices across the school. Further, the cross-grade level or interdisciplinary nature of teams increases collegiality of teachers across groups that would, otherwise, not work together.

## How Can Systems Support the Principles?

From a systems perspective, we do not want to create effective, but isolated teams, which is a typical systems issue in schools. We need to consider the interrelationships among them. Recall the scenario presented for Merryport Middle School at the beginning of the chapter. Teachers did not understand how teams worked together. An empowering strategy for team building is helping teachers understand connections among teams (Boudett & Moody, 2013). In other words, how do teams work together, synergistically, to accomplish the school's work? And, by extension, asks the individual teacher on the team: *What is **my** role in this work?* A starting point to answer this question for members of your school community is to generate a *team connections map*, whereby you can make explicit the relationships among important parts of your overall systems. This graphic can, visually, "explain" a system for your teachers. A simple, sample team connections map is shown in Figure 2.5.

In this example, focused on the critical work of school improvement planning, you might first notice that many of the teams identified in Figure 2.4 are represented. This is purposeful. When many representative teams are engaged, it means that *many—most*—perhaps *all*—of your staff members are actively participating in the overall work. As Michael Fullan asserts to educational leaders in *The NEW Meaning of Educational Change*

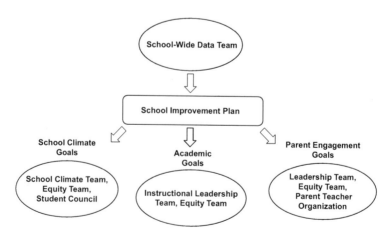

*Figure 2.5* Sample team connections map. Adapted from "We can do this! Transformational leadership for school improvement," by J. D. Visone (2021), in K. N. LaVenia & J. J. May (Eds.), *Case studies in leadership and adult development: Applying theoretical perspectives to real world challenges*. Routledge. Adapted with permission.

(2007), it is through *doing* the work that real change can occur, as opposed to meeting behind closed doors crafting perfectly written theoretical plans. Including many in this distributed leadership effort is empowering, collegial, and impactful (Fullan & Kirtman, 2019).

Logistically, the School-Wide Data Team writes the school improvement plan (more on this later in the chapter), after examining data representing the breadth of the school's assessments and other data sources. Once written, action plans are then sent to other committees, whose charges are to make the action plans come to life. For example, the Instructional Leadership and Equity Teams will focus on the academically focused school improvement goals to plan the professional learning experiences that will meet the needs identified in the action plan and ensure that traditionally marginalized student groups are considered in solutions, respectively. The school climate-based goals are assigned to the School Climate Team, Equity Team, and the Student Council, who will help create solutions and experiences that will meet the demands of the school climate action plan. With a system of teams in operation as shown here, your school can move toward the ideals of the three guiding principles. Many are contributing to leading the school improvement process. A natural effect of this systematic approach is that teachers and other staff members feel they are a part of a true *team*, a desired state of being discussed in Chapter 1. Further, those who feel they are contributing members of a team are empowered and want to do more than those who feel isolated.

I must interject the caveat that some of your team members will still not be able to see the entire figurative forest through the trees, when presented with a team connections map. A means to dig deeper into individual teams' roles is to create a *purpose statement* for each team. If generated collaboratively at the beginning of the school year, team members can leave their first meeting with a clear understanding of what they need to do as a team member and how their group will contribute to overall school success. A sample purpose statement can be found in Figure 2.6.

Notice in the sample purpose statement that the Instructional Leadership Team derives its aims from school touchstones. The mission statement and school improvement process are directly and explicitly connected to the team's work. As leaders, we cannot overcommunicate about connections between what we are doing today and our larger purposes (i.e. mission statement, school goals, vision, etc.). This is because teachers are necessarily consumed by the day-to-day work and do not have the time or forums to

## How Can Systems Support the Principles?

> **Purpose Statement:** *Instructional Leadership Team*
>
> In accordance with our *Mission Statement*:
> - We help our students to experience "rigorous and relevant learning experiences."
> - We help our students to acquire "the knowledge, skills, and attitudes necessary to succeed in a dynamic, competitive global society."
> - We help to ensure that our experiences "challenge students to become active problem solvers and creative, critical thinkers."
>
> In support of our academic *School Improvement Goals*:
> - By focusing on school improvement from an instructional/curricular perspective, we help to maximize our students' learning and growth.
> - By creating professional learning experiences, we help teachers to improve their practice for the benefit of our students' learning.
>
> To accomplish our *purpose*, we:
> - Represent all grade levels/departments in the school.
> - Help set agendas for gradelevel/department meetings, collegial visits, and faculty meetings.
> - Create professional learning experiences that will meet the needs outlined in our school improvement academic goals.
> - Communicate our work back to the staff we represent.

Note that collegial visits are a peer observation structure that will be outlined in Chapter 3.

*Figure 2.6* Sample purpose statement for Instructional Leadership Team. Adapted from "We can do this! Transformational leadership for school improvement," by J. D. Visone (2021), in K. N. LaVenia & J. J. May (Eds.), Case studies in leadership and adult development: Applying theoretical perspectives to real world challenges. Routledge. Adapted with permission.

frequently look at the bigger picture. Staff need to continually hear the *why* behind the actions they are asked to undertake in their practice and within their teams. In a report of their research on influencing public sentiment about education reform efforts, the Frame Works Institute (Bales & O'Neil, 2014) emphasized answering the question of why reforms are needed, since many do not make connections on their own and, in the absence of your connecting the dots, will rely on their own reasoning, which may or may not align with yours. Leaders must help make connections clear, transparent, and real. Also, the purpose statement concretely outlines the charges for the team and, thus, provides a proactive response for the team member who always asks: *Why are we here?* and its closely related cousin, *What are we doing today?* Mental energy can be diverted from perseveration on these questions of purpose and task and applied directly to getting stuff done!

Your teams will also benefit from attending to norms, processes, and roles, as these elements can enhance productivity. Norms are positively worded statements that outline team expectations (Boudett & Moody, 2013). These statements answer questions such as: *What do we expect for premeeting preparation?*, *How will we interact during meetings?*, and *What dispositions characterize productive team function?* Thus, an instructional data team might have a norm that all members will arrive at meetings with their data collected and organized for discussion. A school climate team might espouse that members should always assume positive intentions from fellow members. Norms can engender collegiality by addressing participation expectations, so that all members know that their ideas are valued and important. For example, a norm could be developed whereby each member must comment on decision items. Thus, all voices are heard, even those who might feel intimidated to speak, at first. Also, all members know they will have their turn to share input, which would reduce competition over "air time."

Processes are closely related to norms. These are not always written, but they might answer questions about how the team will function. For example, how will decisions be made? Will the team vote with a simple majority carrying the decision? Perhaps the team will work to build consensus, which is stronger in the long run, but requires more time and energy upfront. If decision making can be somewhat democratic, such as through voting or consensus building, team leaders can further manifest that the group is truly a team, as opposed to a collection of people filling seats and providing "input" to a leader who may or may not pay attention to their ideas (see *Listening 2.0* in Chapter 1 for more information about the power of leadership respecting multiple voices). Finally, when planning for team meetings, consider strategies for active engagement of participants, such as asking team subgroups to complete data reviews and report back to the whole group; asking each member to report on a topic via a whiparound; or having the team jigsaw the creation of a larger product, such as a presentation to be shared with the entire staff. Also, using a system for capturing the business of the team's meeting for later can be helpful, and a minutes format is a frequent structure to capture such information. Minutes for team meetings will be addressed later in this chapter.

## How Can Systems Support the Principles?

Finally, roles can apply a distributed leadership model to a team structure, by enlisting many to assist with team leadership, thus empowering members. One team member or pair of members can be tasked with acting as the facilitator(s) or chair(s), and this role can include creating agendas and leading conversation. These individuals could confer with formal leaders to map out purposes and agendas in advance of meetings. A recorder can be charged with maintaining meeting minutes. A timekeeper can focus the team on the planned agenda. With multiple members sharing these important leadership functions, no one individual is left to juggle all the responsibility.

Team membership is also important. This construct is difficult to prescribe, without knowing the culture, history, contractual obligations, and restrictions of your school. However, in general, it is beneficial to have as many staff members involved (thinking across all your teams) as possible. This is because teachers' capacities are built, and buy-in for teams' collective work can be engendered through participation. Engaged and involved staff members are those who could potentially say their schools embody the three foundational principles. I must note, however, that mere participation is not enough to make team members perceive they are part of a distributed leadership model. The team leadership must "walk the walk" of sharing decision making. As was discussed in the first chapter, this is accomplished in small moments within teams' meetings and work. For example, when Julio brings the Instructional Leadership Team a professional learning suggestion that is connected to the school improvement plan, reasonable, and supported by other teachers on the team—I realize this seems like a big ask, as these are three, specific criteria, but this is a rather typical situation—leadership should find a way to honor and, oftentimes and within reason, *implement* the suggestion. Most teachers bring forward legitimate ideas.

As an exercise to evaluate your present system of teams for completeness and effectiveness, as well as to identify gaps that can be addressed, I offer you the *team system analysis* (see Figure 2.7). With this tool, work together to identify what teams your school includes, what purpose they presently serve, what purposes they *could* serve, how communications flow to and from these teams, and how these teams fit together with each other. Then, determine what gaps you have in your system, after consulting (a) the general list of potential teams identified in Figure 2.4, (b) the rest of this chapter's content, (c) and your own understanding of the school and its

## How Can Systems Support the Principles?

| | | Part I: Your Present Structure | | |
|---|---|---|---|---|
| Team Name | **Who** is on this team? (roles, not people) | What is its **purpose** presently? What could it be? | How does **communication** flow to and from this team? | What **connections** does this team have to other teams and your larger system(s)? |
| | | | | |
| | | | | |
| | | | | |
| | | | | |
| | | | | |

| Part II: What is missing? What solutions can you offer within your existing team structure? |
|---|
| |

| | | Part III: What teams are still needed? | | |
|---|---|---|---|---|
| Potential Team Name | **Who** would be on this team? (roles, not people) | **What need** does this team address? What would be its **purpose**? | How would **communication** flow to and from this team? | What **connections** could this team have to other teams and your larger system(s)? |
| | | | | |
| | | | | |
| | | | | |
| | | | | |

*Figure 2.7* Team system analysis.

needs. An editable, electronic version of this tool can be found in the eResources collection for this book.

Above, I outlined a team system that can empower teachers and invite collegiality through meaningful contributions to the collective work. Communication was referenced as an important variable to consider. Jill Harrison Berg, author of *Leading in Sync: Teacher Leaders and Principals Working Together for Student Learning* (Berg, 2018), wrote about the need for purposeful team systems that have "communications routines" (p. 48) that allow for these teams to function in coordination with each other. I concur, and we shall delve into communications systems next.

## Communications Systems in Support of the Three Foundational Principles

Think back a few pages to the systems thinking questions posed in Figure 2.2. I would like to highlight two of them:

*How does information flow from a meeting to the wider staff?*

*What forum exists for this conversation?*

In order to adequately answer these questions, we need to create two-way systems for communication. We want to have pathways for information to flow that are natural and systematized, rather than haphazard and random. We do not want luck to be a major factor in whether teachers are informed, as was the case for Merryport Middle School's Monica when she asked for help with Freddy. In the context of the teams discussion above, forums for many conversations are potentially created simply by implementing a system of teams. For example, if teachers wish to have a forum to bring forth issues and concerns about curricular matters, having a standing item for roundtable discussion on the Instructional Leadership Team agenda could meet this need. If issues were more related to building safety, representatives to the Security Team could be entrusted to convey these concerns at those meetings on behalf of their grade level or department colleagues, with the understanding that representatives would return with answers for their colleagues.

This forum approach empowers representatives to display a leadership role—advocating for a need and communicating answers back. Further, it requires collegiality, whereby the representatives need to have conversations with colleagues before, during, and after their team meetings. In this approach, the communication system is the *representative herself*, as well as the empowering leadership expectations placed upon her.

However, this representative system is not airtight, since not all representatives are created equally with respect to communication skill. Close your eyes. Imagine the staff member in your school who, though possessing the best intentions, will miscommunicate important details within messages.

## How Can Systems Support the Principles?

Now, picture the colleague who similarly means well, and fully plans to share what happened at the meeting, but just plain forgets. *What? You couldn't think of anyone who matches these descriptions?* I want to work where you do, then! However, if you are like most of us and were able to picture colleagues (or yourself!), these individuals could sink a representative communication system, if that is the *only* mechanism. However, with some strategic leadership, this system can be bolstered to just shy of foolproof.

First, consider providing the representatives with a script to share with colleagues. This is most often manifested in the form of minutes from the team meeting. The representatives could, with the actual team minutes in hand, outline for their colleagues the salient points from the last team meeting. A simple, sample minutes template can be found in Figure 2.8. Second, consider a school-wide forum for communicating the key points and decisions from the team meeting. This will reinforce what your representatives share with their colleagues, serve as a reminder for all that the sharing by representatives needs to occur, and provide a permanent record of the information for your staff. A weekly update email or newsletter could be a forum for this sharing. Finally, whatever communication systems are created, it is wise to strategically identify connections to school goals and priorities, major initiatives, other teams' work, and recent professional learning. Thus, you can continue to link key elements of your system for staff. An editable, electronic version of Figure 2.8 can be found in the eResources collection for this book.

In conclusion, leaders can create a dynamic and effective system of teams. However, without effective systems for communication to match, the

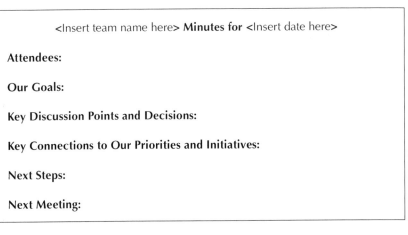

*Figure 2.8* Sample minutes template for a team meeting.

| Communication Systems by Team |||
|---|---|---|
| Team Name | How does **communication** flow to and from this team?* (i.e. representative, minutes, other whole-staff share, archive, etc.) | If communication is not flowing ideally, what **additional communication channels** can you create? |
|  |  |  |
|  |  |  |
|  |  |  |
|  |  |  |
|  |  |  |

*Note.* Communication systems by team were already identified if your team completed the Team System Analysis (Figure 2.7).

*Figure 2.9* Team communication planning worksheet.

teams can still appear to be isolated and disconnected. In Figure 2.9, your team can recall the many communication channels you identified in the Team System Analysis (Figure 2.7), as well as plan to close any communication gaps. Again, an editable, electronic version of Figure 2.9 can be found in the eResources collection for this book. Leaders interested in empowering teacher leadership do well to communicate as transparently as possible, as this clarity of purpose and intent will build upon the trust we examined in Chapter 1 (Fullan & Kirtman, 2019; Tschannen-Moran & Gareis, 2015). Next, we will consider systems related to a very critical function of your teams—school improvement planning.

## School Improvement Planning in Support of the Three Foundational Principles

I know your type. (*I think.*) If you have read this far into this book, you are a leader, whether formally or informally, who seeks a better school for your students and colleagues—a place where all students and adults achieve and feel connected to the work they do. Thus, the concept of school improvement planning is likely not foreign to you. Effective school improvement planning makes use of a systems approach to examining data, determining a

## How Can Systems Support the Principles?

set of priorities and goals, and generating action plans to address the needs identified. Whereas many excellent texts have been devoted to the subject of using data to drive school improvement—the *Data Wise* text referenced earlier (Boudett et al., 2013) is one—my focus will be on the elements of school improvement planning that relate to systems to support empowerment, collegiality, and risk taking. More specifically, I will frame the discussion around team and communications systems.

First, recall Figure 2.5, through which a school can leverage the brainpower and participation of many members of the staff to transact the business of school improvement planning. In Figure 2.5, the School-Wide Data Team creates the school improvement plan. Thus, a representative team from the school (read: *not a principal sitting in her office by herself!*) examines school-wide data, determines priorities, writes improvement goals, creates action plans, and monitors progress. This strategy, enlisting teachers to perform school-wide, data-driven decision making, is consistent with the principles of distributed leadership and serves to build teacher buy-in and empower them as they are sitting at the decision-making table. To guide the work, a format for crafting the school improvement plan can be helpful. Having a physical document capture the work of the School-Wide Data Team as a school improvement plan can aid in a leadership system to share the plan with all stakeholders.

In my work with practicing teachers and administrators, I have seen many formats for school improvement plans (SIPs). However, there are some commonalities that I will share for your consideration. Ideally, the document should include a cover page with general information about the plan: participants who drafted it, the timeframe it covers (i.e. school year[s]), its main goals, etc. Next, the key data used to write the plan could be shared, though some schools and districts prefer to leave the data out, to keep the plan more concise for staff. There is much to be said about keeping improvement plans lean and focused, so they are more accessible and "real" for teachers; overly lengthy and ornate plans do not serve as nimble, living roadmaps for improvement (Fullan, 2007; Fullan & Kirtman, 2019). Quite frankly, hefty plans can be intimidating to staff. Further, to focus on everything is to focus on nothing. Thus, prioritization of a few, high-leverage goals—perhaps, three to six—is recommended.

The action plans, which are where the work can start to come alive for staff, are the crux of the SIP. A solid action plan is headed by a prioritized focus (e.g. reading comprehension, critical thinking skills, social and emotional learning, etc.). I also recommend leadership teams include an equity

## How Can Systems Support the Principles?

lens in school improvement planning, so that this process can help your school see success for *all* students. You might focus your SIP on increasing achievement for a group that has seen less success, or you might argue that, by selecting your chosen focus (e.g. trauma-informed practices), you will be meeting the needs of a vulnerable population. Next, it is helpful to restate the focus in an overarching, broad goal(s), followed by specific SMART (Strategic/Specific, Measurable, Attainable, Results-Based, and Timebound) goals (Conzemius & O'Neill, 2001) that will serve as the yardsticks against which future gains are measured. The action steps themselves are outlined as rows in a table, with details of action steps identified in various columns along each row. Figure 2.10 provides a simple, sample format for school improvement action plans. An editable, electronic version of this template can be found in the eResources collection for this book.

An action plan in this format can serve the communication system, which is where I would like to focus our attention. As stated above, the inclusion of many in the creation and monitoring of the plan (through the School-Wide Data Team) is one way to empower and engender collegiality. Further, this empowerment can be magnified, when the system of teams (i.e. Instructional Leadership Team, Equity Team, Leadership Team, Parent Teacher Organization, Student Council, etc.) is enlisted to operationalize

---

**Action Plan Focus**
(*What is our priority?*):

**Equity Lens**
(*How will our focus promote success for* all *students?*):

**Broad School Goal**
(*What are we trying to accomplish? [without numbers, just skills and/or outcomes]*):

**SMART Goal(s)**
(*What are our specific, numeric targets? [from baseline scores to targets]*):

| Action Step Description | Resources Needed | Timeframe | Roles Involved | Monitoring Evidence |
|---|---|---|---|---|
|  |  |  |  |  |

*Figure 2.10* Sample school improvement action plan template.

## How Can Systems Support the Principles?

the various action plans (i.e. academic, school climate, parent engagement, etc.). However, one must not forget about the remainder of school staff and other stakeholders who had not participated on any of these teams. *How will **all** staff members be brought into the work of the SIP?*

Before answering this question, I will share a non-example from my work with aspiring school leaders. I will often poll my classes informally about whether they have seen their own school's improvement plan. It is typical and consistent for about half of the students—all teachers and other actively employed certified educators—to keep their hands in their laps, meaning that many teachers never see the school improvement plans that are supposed to drive their work! A big mistake many formal leaders make is keeping the school's improvement plan to themselves and their Leadership/School-Wide Data Teams. This approach, while possibly empowering to members of these two teams, misses an opportunity to increase the empowerment and collegiality for many others in the school. Thus, a system of communication and engagement with the plan is in order.

Key points of interaction with all staff members should include: after a draft is written, when a school year begins, and when key data points are evaluated against the plan. A logical starting place is shortly after the School-Wide Data Team writes the first draft of the plan, which, if end-of-year data are used as baseline scores for the following year's work, occurs shortly before the school year ends in the spring. Note the implication here (see the phrase: *first draft*) that the initial version of the plan might not actually be the final version. *You mean we actually have to read this plan and interact with it after it is written?* Yes! Shortly after the first draft is created by the School-Wide Data Team, create a forum for staff members to read the plan and offer their feedback. This could occur at a faculty meeting, a series of PLC meetings, or even online, so long as the purposes are for staff members to familiarize themselves with the document and offer feedback. The feedback is then returned to the School-Wide Data Team so revisions can be made.

The next logical point for whole-school interaction with the plan is as the school year begins. The now-revised plan can be provided to PLCs for the purpose of teams and individual educators reconnecting with the plan and determining how their own teaching and/or work will contribute to it. Finally, throughout the year (say, three times), members of the School-Wide Data Team examine data that indicate the school's progression with respect to SIP goals. The team members can work in subgroups to create a presentation for the entire staff about the status of SIP efforts. This presentation,

## How Can Systems Support the Principles?

which is then shared with the entire staff, perhaps at a faculty meeting or PLCs, would include:

- status of SIP goals with respect to the most recent data (e.g. *We want 75% of our students to attain a particular proficiency level. As of the fall assessments, we have 68%. We are getting there, but we have some work left to do!*);
- status with respect to action plan steps (e.g. *We have completed the action step with respect to _____, while we still must complete _____, _____, and _____*).

This school improvement system will build collegiality through collective work during PLCs on goal progress, and empowerment will be realized for those who helped to create and present the plan. Figure 2.11 shows a potential timeline and system for school improvement work that engages the entire school.

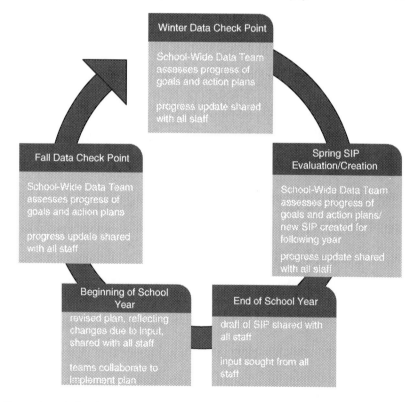

*Figure 2.11* School improvement plan (SIP) timeline to maximize engagement and support the three foundational principles.

A final communication vehicle to immerse your staff in school improvement work and further empower their engagement in the process is to include many messages about the SIP throughout other parts of your system. For example, if you craft regular communications to your entire staff or small groups, include school goals as a standing item in a prominent place. For example, a text box with your three school goals in an upper corner of your weekly newsletter/memo to staff can keep these guiding foci at the fore of everyone's mind. Posters with school goals in meeting areas are another way to increase the number of times staff members view these goals. Repetition will ensure staff do not lose sight of what your team is trying to collectively accomplish. Finally, at the start of every professional learning workshop, faculty meeting, and other meeting of importance, connect the purpose and agenda of the session to the school improvement plan. Thus, all will begin to see that every effort is moving the group toward the same place. No one will be able to say: *Why are we doing this?* I should note, as this chapter comes to a close, that the systems-based strategies I just applied to school improvement planning can analogously be applied to other school-wide needs, such as planning a budget, creating a common vision, increasing equitable access for all students, writing accreditation reports, to name a few.

## Summary

Creating effective, participative systems within your school can empower staff members, engender collegiality, and encourage responsible risk taking. To follow a systems approach in a school means to understand that, for the school to function effectively, there are many elements to consider. By altering one aspect of the system, other elements will be affected. Key questions to consider from a systems perspective in schools include:

How does information flow from a meeting to the wider staff?
What are the connections among different teams and committees within the school, and how do these pieces fit together?
How does this process work here at our school?
What is the chain of command for this issue?
What forum exists for this conversation?

> If this happens, how will it affect other things?
> Who is involved in making which decisions?
> Who initiates this process?
> What is the timeline for this to happen?
> How can we work more efficiently?
> What are different individuals' roles in that situation?
> What is the purpose of this action/team/committee?
> What is the root cause of this situation?
> What strategic action can address this particular problem?
> How does this situation look from different vantage points within the school?

In order to provide appropriate answers to these questions, various aspects of the school's functions should be considered. Scheduling can be maximized for teacher collaboration, including through the provision of common planning time. A system of teams can create forums for distributed leadership, empowerment, and collegiality. A system of teams in your school can break the complex work of schools into manageable portions, as well as engage all your staff in the work. Communication systems must be employed effectively to allow for two-way flow of information. School improvement planning is an overarching process that can provide many opportunities for staff collegiality and leadership. If a system for school improvement planning is strategically designed, staff members can be maximally engaged in the process, empowering them.

## Questions to Consider for Chapter 2:
### How Can Our Systems Support the Three Foundational Principles?

1. Think about the systems in your school. How many of them can you identify readily? Of these, how many are functioning well? Not so well?
2. Recall past situations where changes to aspects of a system

affected other aspects. Were these resulting changes positive or negative?
3. Complete the team system analysis in Figure 2.7. Does your school have a system of teams that meets the team needs identified in Figure 2.4? More importantly, do your teams meet your school's needs?
4. Do staff members on your various teams and committees understand their purpose as members of these groups? Can they articulate their connections to the other teams and the larger purposes of the school? If not, how can this situation be improved?
5. Examine the team communication planning worksheet (Figure 2.9). Evaluate the status of your teams' communication systems. What is working well? What needs to change?
6. Assess the effectiveness of your system for school improvement. Who is engaged in the process? Who is not? How can you get those who are not engaged to be so?
7. What are your own takeaways from this chapter? What is a tangible next step for you and your school toward the ideal of creating systems that will empower, increase collegiality, and promote risk taking?

# References

Bales, S. N., & O'Neil, M. (2014). *Putting it back together again: Reframing education using a core story approach.* Frame Works Institute.

Berg, J. H. (2018). *Leading in sync: Teacher leaders and principals working together for student learning.* ASCD.

Boudett, K. P., City, E. A., & Murnane, R. J. (Eds.). (2013). *Data wise: A step-by-step guide to using assessment results to improve teaching and learning* (Rev. ed.). Harvard Education Press.

Boudett, K. P., & Moody, L. (2013). Organizing for collaborative work. In K. P. Boudett, E. A. City, & R. J. Murnane (Eds.), *Data wise: A step-by-step guide to using assessment results to improve teaching and learning* (Rev. ed., pp. 13–34). Harvard Education Press.

Conzemius, A., & O'Neill, J. (2001). *Building shared responsibility for student learning.* ASCD.

Diamond, J. B., & Spillane, J. P. (2016). School leadership and management from a distributed perspective: A 2016 retrospective and prospective. *Management in Education, 30*(4), 147–154. https://doi.org/10.1177/0892020616665938

Drago-Severson, E., & Blum-DeStefano, J. (2018). *Leading change together: Developing educator capacity within schools and systems.* ASCD.

Fullan, M. (2007). *The NEW meaning of educational change* (4th ed.). Teachers College Press.

Fullan, M., & Kirtman, L. (2019). *Coherent school leadership: Forging clarity from complexity.* ASCD.

Hall, G. E., & Hord, S. M. (2019). *Implementing change: Patterns, principles, and potholes* (5th ed.). Pearson.

Leithwood, K., Louis, K. S., Anderson, S., & Wahlstrom, K. (2004). *Review of research: How leadership influences student learning.* The Wallace Foundation. https://doi.org/10.1007/978-90-481-2660-6

Meadows, D. (2008). *Thinking in systems: A primer.* Chelsea Green.

Spillane, J. P. (2006). *Distributed leadership.* Jossey-Bass.

Spillane, J. P., Halverson, R., & Diamond, J. B. (2001). Investigating school leadership practice: A distributed perspective. *Educational Researcher, 30*(3), 23–28. http://www.jstor.org/stable/3594470

Stroh, D. P. (2015). *Systems thinking for social change: A practical guide to solving complex problems, avoiding unintended consequences, and achieving lasting results.* Chelsea Green.

Tschannen-Moran, M., & Gareis, C. R. (2015). Principals, trust, and cultivating vibrant schools. *Societies, 5,* 256–276. https://doi.org/10.3390/soc5020256

Visone, J. D. (2021). We can do this! Transformational leadership for school improvement. In K. N. LaVenia & J. J. May (Eds.), *Case studies in leadership and adult development: Applying theoretical perspectives to real world challenges.* Routledge.

# The Power of "Seeing It"
## The Collegial Visit

The time is ticking away from Period 4, which means that teachers in the Fairview Middle School Grade 7 Language Arts Professional Learning Community had less than 10 minutes to solidify next week's implementation plan about close reading of informational text. Cheryl had a solid plan. She had used this sequence of lessons in the past, and it had produced some excellent gains for her students. To help her colleagues "see" what she had done for these lessons, she brought hard copies of a worksheet she used to teach close reading skills explicitly. However, it quickly became apparent that this method of sharing would not result in the other teachers internalizing Cheryl's strategies for these lessons.

"I am not sure what I am looking at here, Cheryl," stated Jasmin. The given artifact was an inadequate representation of the planning, on-the-fly adjustments, and differentiation Cheryl regularly employs to extract great value from this lesson sequence.

"Well, I think you would put the kids into groups, and they would work together to get the top portion done, right?" offered Pam.

"Yeah, but how will the groups know what to do? Is this an inquiry exercise?" Jasmin probed.

"I'm not sure about that," answered Pam.

"Actually, you both have some good ideas, but this is how I actually conduct this sequence … "

Cheryl proceeded to outline her lesson plan, in a procedural fashion, as the team listened intently. Despite their best intentions, details were forgotten, and shades of meaning and nuance were lost in "translation." Jasmin, though her concrete questions were answered, was no closer to truly understanding how Cheryl taught this lesson sequence, since she knew that Cheryl's delivery of the content is as important as the procedural steps

DOI: 10.4324/9781003190370-3

and materials used. More importantly, Jasmin's students would not benefit from her lessons in the same manner that Cheryl's did. This is because Jasmin did not know about an effective hook that Cheryl had perfected after several attempts, nor would she know how to probe students' thinking with examples and follow-up questions the way Cheryl did. Jasmin was not a novice or ineffective teacher. On the contrary, Jasmin was a dedicated, seasoned teacher, and she was genuinely interested in implementing the effective sequence of lessons Cheryl had created and shared with the group. Jasmin, along with her teammates, had agreed to adopt Cheryl's strategies and lessons to help their students more effectively consume informational text. However, other than Cheryl, they would all fall short of Cheryl's usual level of effectiveness.

If only Cheryl's teammates could have seen how these lessons unfolded …

The Fairview Middle School Grade 7 Language Arts PLC situation is a typical one. After all, there is a very significant logistical barrier preventing teachers from being able to see their colleagues teach—*students*! Necessarily, teachers are with students most of their working day, between teaching, monitoring homerooms, serving at duty posts, providing extra help, proctoring study halls, and offering support and advice for the plethora of situations that students bring to them—all with barely enough time to inhale a quick lunch, use the restroom once (or twice, *but don't get greedy* …), and make a modicum of photocopies. Thus, there is little room for teachers to catch that great strategy a colleague has mentioned, though that colleague might literally be teaching in the adjacent classroom! It is a problem as old as schools. Since teachers' primary responsibility is to teach students, their ability to collaborate and learn from one another in real time suffers.

Renowned, late educational leadership thinker Richard Elmore framed some of this challenge aptly, referring to the isolation of teachers within the profession (Elmore, 2000, 2005). Teachers, he explained, generally work by themselves, behind their classroom doors, largely unaware of the great or deficient teaching that exists on the other side of the wall from them. Further, due to the "loose coupling" of the educational system (Elmore, 2000, p. 5), whereby administrators have neither the time nor the real authority to require specific practices, there is little ability to bring the great practices occurring in Ms. Dynamo's Room 302 to scale across the entire grade level or department, much less the entire school. In sum, schools are frequently handicapped by the structure of individual actors/teachers operating independently.

This pessimistic image of teachers working in isolation behind closed doors for seemingly endless hours without significant opportunities to interact with other adults might be an extreme and outdated view—*or it might just describe your school.* Either way, the image stands in stark contrast from the ideal of a learning organization, which was outlined in a foundational work from outside the field of education by Peter Senge (1990) called *The Fifth Discipline: The Art and Practice of the Learning Organization.* Senge challenged organizations to learn together, whereby the organization would become more than just production or an end result, and the process of learning to do the work better was an integral component of success. Partially due to Senge's book, the field of education has been transforming into one that has recognized that working together is imperative to maximize results for our students.

## The Case for Teachers to Learn from One Another's Work

Across the profession, many have called for leaders to create and maintain systems for teachers to work together for the common purpose of raising student achievement. Whether these efforts are under the umbrella of data-driven decision making (Boudett & Moody, 2013; D. B. Reeves, 2009; Ronka, 2007) or, perhaps, professional learning communities (DuFour et al., 2010; DuFour & Eaker, 1998; DuFour & Marzano, 2011; Eaker & Keating, 2012), the emphasis on group processes for improving what teachers do to impact student success is clear. Further, many authors have specifically called for teachers to learn by observing their peers (Bambrick-Santoyo, 2019; City et al., 2005; Garet et al., 2001; Hoerr, 2016; Kaufman, 2007; Learning Forward, 2017; Stinson, 2017), as this type of learning is strongly aligned with research about effective professional learning, which should be collaborative, job-embedded, deeply connected to teachers' daily work, on-going throughout the year, and utilizing teachers' expertise (Croft et al., 2010; Garet et al., 2001; Learning Forward, 2017; National Archives and Records Administration, 2009; Penuel et al., 2007; Wei et al., 2010). Further, spending time observing the work of peers has been found to increase teachers' job satisfaction (P. M. Reeves et al., 2017; Schleicher, 2016). How then, does this "reform" type of professional learning translate to improved practices? You might logically ask: *Why should we invest significant energy in doing things in this very different and hands-on manner?*

The first reason to shift toward teachers learning by observing each other's practice comes from an influential study by the RAND corporation (Johnston & Tsai, 2018). The authors conducted a survey of more than 1,800 teachers across the United States regarding their collaboration practices. The positive findings included that about 96% of the respondents reported collaborating with their colleagues about instructional matters, and nearly half did so on a weekly or more frequent basis. These data point to movement within the profession away from Elmore's (2000, 2005) challenge of isolation of practice. However, and critically relevant to this discussion, of the collaboration forms addressed by the survey (i.e. discussions about instructional practices, common analysis of data, and peer observations), peer observations were the *least common format* identified by teachers, with 44% of teachers indicating that they had never been observed by a colleague or vice versa to share teaching practices. This is an unfortunate finding, given the many wonderful teaching practices occurring in a typical school. The fact that other educators do not benefit from seeing these practices is borderline negligent. Clearly, there is much room for growth with peer observation as a learning vehicle. Further, the report provided some positivity with respect to a path forward, as teachers who were provided with more opportunities to collaborate, did, in fact, report more collaboration. Thus, if leadership teams build systems to conduct peer observations, they can and will happen.

As a theoretical lens, the *professional capital* framework of Andy Hargreaves and Michael Fullan (2012, 2013) underscores the need for working together for common goals and is a solid starting point to answer the question about why this work is important. Their theory includes a formula of constructs, whereby human capital, plus social capital, plus decisional capital, yields professional capital. The authors explained that *human capital* refers to the learning and skillsets of individual teachers. Clearly, it benefits your school's students if individual teachers are learning more and can do more (Baumert et al., 2010). However, this individualized approach, which is targeted by traditional professional learning structures (i.e. workshops, professional reading, outside presenters, conferences, working with instructional coaches, etc.) will not completely address Elmore's identified challenge of scale. There is much greater potential within a school that utilizes group learning to advance the collective expertise of all teachers (DeWitt, 2017). This is where *social capital* comes into play.

Social capital was defined by the authors as the complete set of interactions among members of a group (in this case, teachers). Healthy social capital relies, in part, on the teacher self-efficacy (TSE) increase that can be obtained through the verbal persuasion of more experienced others (Bandura, 1977, 1997). TSE, of course, is a teacher's general belief that she can affect student results (Guskey & Passaro, 1994; Klassen et al., 2011; Ross, 2013; Tschannen-Moran et al., 1998). TSE refers to a teacher's confidence that her efforts in planning, differentiating, and cajoling will, in fact, result in student learning. Teachers who are learning from others in their midst, particularly those with more experience or who regularly yield the best student results, can leave collaborative settings with greater efficacy that they, too, can achieve more for their students. Research from the Organisation for Economic Co-operation and Development (OECD; Schleicher, 2016), an international organization of 38 nations that works to shape international policy across different fields, including education (OECD, n.d.), reported that teachers who learn collaboratively, including through observing peers' instruction and providing feedback, display increased TSE. As a bonus, these teachers also reported higher job satisfaction along with their increased confidence. Work is more fun when you believe you can make a difference!

Research by Carrie Leana (2011) succinctly pushes us past the reliance on the human capital model for improvement. Specifically, in schools with higher degrees of social capital (i.e. trusting inter-teacher relationships, increased collaboration, etc.), *students learn more*. Further, for teachers with lower levels of individual human capital, working in a school with a high degree of social capital can increase their individual effectiveness to near-average levels. Let me express this important conclusion in a different way. In your own school, considering Elmore's issue of scale, think of the least effective teachers. Likely much effort is exerted by administrators, coaches, teacher leaders, and central office personnel to improve these teachers' practices. However, if these teachers simply work within teams, grade levels, or departments/schools that are highly collaborative and trusting, these teachers can improve—and even perform as well as the *average-performing teachers* in their midst, all the while using "existing resources," which is a euphemism for not costing your district's taxpayers any more money!

The final of the three legs of the professional capital stool is *decisional capital*, which refers to teachers' ability to make decisions, in light of their learning through varied experiences (Hargreaves & Fullan, 2012, 2013). These experiences can include teachers' own instruction, but, more relevantly here, they include social capital interactions, where teachers learn from one another. Even more relevantly, the authors assert that teachers seeing each other's instruction can increase decisional capital. Contrary to our example of Fairview Middle School, the ability to see the delivery of instruction by their peers can push teachers' own capabilities and confidence in their lesson planning.

International research also supports the power of collective learning and, in particular, peer observation. Hargreaves and O'Connor (2018) studied collaboration efforts in five different settings around the world to determine the elements of their construct *collaborative professionalism*. Among their findings were that collaborative professionalism includes collaborative inquiry, collective responsibility, collective initiative, mutual dialogue, and joint work, among other characteristics. It is not much of a stretch to apply these concepts to peer observation. We will examine how peer observations can be used to test new instructional ideas and experiment (recall risk taking as one of this book's guiding principles). The ability to examine instruction and discuss it, collaboratively, will certainly move your groups toward collective responsibility, as the focus of this joint work and dialogue shifts from students in individual teachers' classrooms to learners across classrooms.

I would be remiss not to mention the role of Bandura's (1986) social learning theory in presenting my case for teachers viewing each other's instruction. As Bandura outlined, a powerful learning vehicle is imitation. Without the observation of action, imitation is nothing more than an educated guess. Witnessing instructional practice, firsthand, allows for more accurate imitation for social learning. Further, having the benefit of a more-experienced peer displaying an example of instructional practice can help a teacher advance her own skills beyond her present *zone of proximal development*, that "sweet spot" in any learning process, where a learner is challenged beyond what she can presently do, but with enough support that the challenge does not overwhelm or frustrate (Vygotsky, 1978).

Some related professional learning models that apply social learning theory can be instructive here, as well. Namely, teachers watching videotaped lessons for professional learning were later found to effectively implement the viewed practices in their own instruction (Tekkumru-Kisa et al., 2018). Also, co-teaching has recently been framed as a vehicle for regular and special education teachers to learn through watching each other's practice (Jung et al., 2019), whereby general education teachers learn about research-based inclusion strategies, and special education teachers gain a deeper understanding of regular education curricula and strategies.

If consideration of theory and related research was not convincing enough that teachers should be viewing each other's instruction as an efficient way to drive improvement with existing resources, consider these more practical connections. First, ponder this finding from some of my own research with United States National Blue Ribbon Schools: many of these exceedingly effective schools, recognized as high achieving by their respective states, make a practice of teachers viewing each other's instruction (Visone, 2018). Second, in studying schools implementing a structure for peer observation known as collegial visits, teachers have consistently outlined their affinity for the process (Visone, 2019, 2020)—Read: *They like it!*—sharing that this learning vehicle is more authentic than traditional approaches, and seeing a lesson delivered is so much more powerful than just reading or talking about it. Further, teachers came to view their colleagues as resources, while building their own confidence about what they can offer to the team. Further still, collegial visits have been shown through my own research to enhance the school's overall social capital (Visone, 2019). Teachers directly gained discrete skills and pedagogical strategies from their peers, and they were more likely to seek out their colleagues for assistance in the future. They also used their learning from one another to tighten the instructional consistency across different classrooms, and their collective accountability and commitment to each other and their students increased. Additionally, and most importantly, teachers' instructional practices improved (as evidenced by administrative walkthrough scores) in the areas of focus for the visits, displaying the visits' power in refining teaching practice.

Second, I have the pleasure of presenting annually about collegial visits with a teacher leader without a formal title, Melissa Bornas, who teaches second grade at Anna Reynolds Elementary School in Newington, CT, where I had proudly served as principal. She shares with our annual audience of teachers and administrators what a system of collegial visits can do for teachers, including affirming and refining their instructional practices, building teachers' confidence (recall the earlier discussion of TSE in this chapter), and improving collaboration. Further, the practice of learning alongside colleagues in an authentic way can foster a collective ownership of the success of all children in the school, not just the children in individual teachers' classrooms. Finally, she shares that this process helps to create a collaborative leadership mentality, which is both a rationale for and goal of teacher leadership. In her own words, she shared with me:

> Through the practice of collegial visits, I was able to evolve my teaching practices, specifically understanding how strong collaboration and "letting other educators in" can promote student growth beyond this one observation. It opens the door to conversations … The practice of collegial visits gives classroom teachers the opportunity to learn from one another and lead. It promotes leadership among all, even those who may not have seen themselves as a leader prior. It creates a feeling of unmeasurable success, belonging, and job satisfaction.
>
> (M. Bornas, personal communication, April 30, 2021)

Finally, I conclude my rationale for peer observation in the form of collegial visits with this pair of illustrative anecdotes. As a principal, I facilitated the monthly meetings of my Instructional Leadership Team, which was part of our foundational system of teams described in Chapter 2. At one meeting, a respected teacher leader in our school, having recently heard another respected teacher leader describing a specific and effective teaching strategy, shared a wonder that is repeated so often in schools. *I wish I could see what she does in her classroom.* If you help to create a culture and system where teachers can regularly expect to learn from one another and view each other's instruction, this question will no longer need to be asked. The question served as a pivotal moment for our school to create a system of *collegial visits*, our structure for common viewing of instruction.

Second, fast-forwarding a few years, I entered a classroom to conduct an informal observation of a teacher. Upon locating a seat from which I could observe the goings-on, I spotted another teacher in the back of the room. When I asked this visiting teacher why she was in the classroom, she stated that the observed, younger teacher was quite skilled at a certain pedagogical strategy, and the visiting teacher wanted to see the strategy in action. Importantly, the *visiting veteran teacher* routinely earned the highest student achievement scores in the building. So, one of the strongest veteran teachers in the school was willing to learn from a much-less-veteran colleague by visiting the younger colleague's classroom. That is when I knew our culture had truly shifted.

At this point, you are likely wondering: *Okay, but how can we actually do this work?* I'm so glad you asked! We consider the *what* and *how* of collegial visits next.

## Collegial Visits: *What?*

Unlike creating the supportive cultural conditions that undergird this type of collaborative work, the protocol for collegial visits is not complicated (Visone, 2016, 2019, 2020). Collegial visits are focused on an aspect of instruction relevant to the school or a smaller subunit (i.e. grade level, department, vertical team, etc.). The focus should be known weeks, or even months, in advance of the visit to allow for the host teacher to experiment and take risks to acquire new skills. The focus represents the purpose for learning, which one would expect in any professional learning structure. One of the teachers in the group volunteers to host her colleagues in her classroom, as well as any other relevant personnel who can benefit from the experience, such as coaches, support personnel, and, even, administrators. *Wait! Hold on. Did you just say "administrators," Jeremy?!* Yes, I did. This is not a typo. The decision to include administrators, who benefit greatly from the collegial sharing process, is discussed a bit later in this chapter. Stay tuned.

To maximize learning during the visit, create a set of guiding questions, preferably collaboratively. All visiting staff members should have a copy of the guiding questions with them as they observe. The viewed lesson should be long enough to see a complete concept taught (perhaps close to 30 minutes). Finally, following the visit to the host teacher's classroom, the entire team, *including the host teacher*, debriefs together to share reflections about the lesson and implications for all participants' classrooms.

It should be noted that collegial visits are only one of many existing protocols available for the common viewing of instruction. However, the collegial visits model was designed to take advantage of positive features of some of these models, while strategically avoiding specific other features. For example, one of the most popular models for common viewing of teaching is the instructional rounds model (City et al., 2009). In practice, rounds include a visiting team, but the team typically observes many classrooms in a day, which results in visits that are rather short, sometimes as finite as 10 minutes. Also, the rounds model does not usually include host teachers in debriefing sessions, and individualized feedback to host teachers is often absent. This can leave a host teacher continually second-guessing herself, wondering what her colleagues or administrators thought about her lesson. After all, an observation of practice without feedback does not help improve a teacher's instructional practice (Sterrett, 2015). Feedback in the collegial visits model is provided to host teachers through debriefing sessions. No longer will a host teacher be left to wonder about others' impressions of her teaching. Details of the collegial visits protocol will be explained in greater detail later in this chapter, following some reminders about the cultural prerequisites for this type of work.

## Collegial Visits: *How?*

When helping schools create systems of collegial visits, I emphasize—if those leading the work do not realize these truths for themselves!—the importance of creating a fertile foundation through culture building and engendering buy in with teachers. Having a truly collaborative culture will include teachers serving as resources for each other (Fullan & Kirtman, 2019). However, having teachers enter each other's classrooms is not light work that will be immediately accepted and seen as valuable in all school settings. As mentioned in the first two chapters, foundations must be set. These include a culture driven by that same trio of principles that will forge a strong social capital base of trusting relationships and collegiality. Again, these principles are:

(a) **empowerment**: Our staff members feel competent and believe that they are equipped to make decisions in the best interest of our students and school. Our teachers have sound ideas that can improve what we do. (If this one sounds familiar, note the logical connection to decisional capital.);

(b) **collegiality**: Our staff works together to solve problems of practice. We do not work in isolation. What we learn, we share. (Here, think professional learning communities and social capital.); and,

(c) **risk taking**: We do not advance if we do not try new things and experiment. We are not afraid to do things differently. (This last principle speaks to the trusting relationships required for social capital to develop. Further, it is manifested by the willingness of teachers to open their classroom doors to colleagues and their openness to experiment with new instructional practices.)

The three foundational principles are shown again in Figure 3.1.

Further, there must be a cultural norm that peers will view experimentation positively. More importantly, formal leaders reinforce risk taking when teachers' innovative ideas to improve practice are supported—within reason, of course. Ultimately, if teachers are successful at improving student learning, there is little need to argue about aesthetics. However, if practices are not successful, the conversation to discontinue them is not personal, but practical. These principles should not only be espoused by formal leaders but also lived in the daily small moments that define teachers' opinions.

Building buy in from staff is more complicated to achieve. Fullan (2007) implored facilitators of change to engage people's emotions to help move their thinking. Reeves (2009) suggested that early wins are key to gaining support and momentum for change. I would agree with both suggestions, and, to meet these ideals, leaders must keep the conversation and experience maximally positive and devoid of negatively judgmental behavior, both from viewing peers and leaders, particularly in the early stages of your school's evolution to this type of collaborative work. Practically, collegial visits should focus upon professional learning needs in the school (i.e. what you are working on *now* in the building; recall the need for professional learning to connect deeply to the daily work of teachers), and professional learning should be the *only* goal of the visits. This tenet is so important that I will write it again: *collegial visits are about professional learning, only.*

This professional learning aim is diametrically opposed to an evaluation focus. In some states, teacher evaluation has become a source of frustration

| | |
|---|---|
| **empowerment** | Our staff members feel competent and believe that they are equipped to make decisions in the best interest of our students and school. Our teachers have sound ideas that can improve what we do. |
| **collegiality** | Our staff works together to solve problems of practice. We do not work in isolation. What we learn, we share. |
| **risk taking** | We do not advance if we do not try new things and experiment. We are not afraid to do things differently. |

*Figure 3.1* The three foundational principles to empower teacher leadership

for teachers (Donaldson, 2016; Liu et al., 2019), due to teachers' and leaders' increased workloads, shifts in teachers' work away from what they believe they should be doing, perceived validity issues within the systems, and the utility (or lack thereof) of feedback received (or *not* received) from formal leaders. In spite of teacher evaluation systems being designed for objectivity and evidence, there is inherently judgment involved, and judgment is a mindset and connotation you will want to avoid, if you expect teachers to feel comfortable teaching in front of their peers. It is certainly possible, with high levels of social capital, after implementing collegial visits for a period of time, that schools can permit more critical conversations that push teachers beyond their comfort zones. However, to achieve early wins, I recommend keeping the conversations complimentary, appreciative, and positive for the host teachers. The critical component can be situated in a discussion about the next steps for all participants. *How will what you saw today influence your practice?* Further, messaging should emphasize that collegial visits *are just another professional learning vehicle*, like workshops, grade level/department meetings, webinars, professional reading, etc. They are not a new "thing" onto themselves. This angle can assuage the ever-skeptical *Oh, here comes one more thing!* crowd that can make faculty meetings and implementing change so much fun for leaders. Keep the focus always on the *learning*, not the visits.

Beyond cultural foundations, many logistics are involved in planning collegial visits for professional learning. These include determining foci for the visits, assembling a visiting team to participate, creating guiding questions, scheduling so that teachers are available at the same time, and facilitating the visits and debriefing sessions. These considerations are outlined next.

## Determining the Foci for Collegial Visits

As stated above, collegial visits should not be considered an initiative by themselves; they exist solely as a professional learning vehicle, and, as such, are beholden to your school's learning needs. Logically, if you have a solid system to enhance student learning as described in Chapter 2, your school is likely operating under a school improvement plan. If so, this document can serve as the source of staff learning needs for collegial visits. When I was a principal, the school improvement plan was almost always the source of foci for our collegial visits. By circling back to the school improvement plan, you show your commitment to (a) maintaining focus on a few important constructs for improvement (Read: *This is not another thing—collegial visits will help us with that other thing we are already working toward!*) and (b) coherence among your many efforts, something we can never provide enough for our staff. If your school improvement plan either (a) is not the logical place to find professional learning priorities for your school or, more importantly, (b) *does not exist* (I am so sorry to hear this, though Chapter 2 provides a model to use for this work!), other sources of potential foci could be district-wide improvement plans or professional learning calendars that outline plans for adult learning throughout the school year.

Selecting foci for collegial visits should be a collaborative enterprise. Considering the importance of participant buy in, teaching staff should have a significant say in what their teams will learn from each other. To harken back to Chapter 2 and its recommendation for a system of teams, a team devoted to your school's professional learning needs would be a logical group to undertake this challenge. Perhaps, share action plans from the school improvement plan with your team and pose the question: *Instructional Leadership Team, as you can see, we are focused this year on X, Y, and Z for our professional learning needs. Of these topics, which one would our teams benefit from seeing most/first/now?*

The decision about a focus might also be influenced by what can reasonably be observed within a lesson and/or whether seeing a construct in action is necessary for teacher learning to occur. For example, your team might determine that interventions for students functioning significantly below grade level are not an ideal focus for collegial visits, as these strategies occur over the course of time and, as such, are often difficult to witness within a single lesson. On the other hand, if your school is focusing on the rigor level of questioning posed to students, this construct is easily viewed during lessons, and there is definitely a delivery aspect to questioning students that is difficult to replicate during a discussion in a conference room. There are nuances to feedback given, probing questions to follow up student responses, scaffolding, and timing considerations that cannot be explained easily outside the context of a classroom. Thus, the rigor of questioning would make a fine focus for a round of collegial visits. To provide some tangible ideas for this abstract discussion, a *rather incomplete* list

| | |
|---|---|
| differentiation | classroom climate-building strategies |
| a specific, research-based instructional strategy | small-group instruction |
| implementation of new standards | implementation of new curricular resources |
| questioning strategies | assessment practices |
| restorative practices | rigor in questioning, activities, assessment, etc. |
| problem-based teaching | student independence/ownership over learning |
| student engagement | common language |
| workstations | gamification |
| classroom management | workshop model of instruction |
| teaching in a virtual/hybrid model | social and emotional learning |

*Note.* Did I mention that this list is not exhaustive? You will need to identify foci to meet the specific learning needs of your school's adults.

*Figure 3.2* Potential foci for collegial visits.

of potential collegial visit foci can be found in Figure 3.2. These topics are broad, as I don't know the specific learning needs of your school, so you will need to tailor these ideas (or your own team's ideas, preferably) to meet your school's needs.

The decision about a focus might also be individualized by teams, rather than for the entire school. I have witnessed situations where teams have asked their leaders to utilize collegial visits for a specific topic they were examining as a team, such as implementing a curricular change that might not be relevant to the entire school. From my vantage point, the closer the focus of the visit is to the daily work of teachers on that team, the greater the buy in and deeper the learning.

## Determining the Collegial Visits Unit of Analysis and Team

In order to maximize learning during collegial visits and minimize wasted time for any stakeholders, participating teams should be strategically constructed. The first question that must be answered is: *What is the unit of analysis for this set of collegial visits?* Ultimately, the teams for collegial visits, like professional learning communities, should consist of educators with a common instructional focus, such as a grade level or departmental team. Logically, you will want people participating in the visit and around the debriefing table who are all speaking the same language and who have the same interest in the chosen instructional focus. As chosen foci for visits change, so could the most logical strategic group to participate. For example, when you examine a specific curricular change or instructional strategy that is unique to a grade level or content area (e.g. a Next Generation Science Standards life science disciplinary core idea), it makes sense to create grade level (for elementary schools) or departmental (for secondary schools) teams. If you focus on a construct relevant across grade levels (e.g. writing a persuasive essay), it might be logical to create a vertical team. Finally, if your focus has universal interest across not only grade levels but also content areas (e.g. questioning strategies, rigor in learning activities, restorative practices, culturally relevant pedagogy, social and emotional learning, virtual instruction, etc.), you might wish to create a heterogeneous, interdisciplinary group of teachers from across the school. Note that leaders should consider group dynamics when constructing visiting teams. It is possible to reap the benefits of collegial visits with as few as one visitor and as many as eight. I would not recommend having more than eight members of a visiting team, both due to the large number of adults descending upon one classroom and also to allow for greater conversation flow in the debriefing session after the visit.

Once you have determined the group of teachers that will comprise the core of the collegial visits team, you must decide what other staff members should be invited. Again, being strategic with these selections, in advance of the visits, will avoid wasted time or hurt feelings later. Do you want, for example, your interventionists to see how classroom teachers address a curricular concept, so they can reinforce this learning in their small-group and individual lessons? Do you want your instructional coaches or resource teachers to participate in the visits, either for the benefit of their own professional learning or to help deliver the host teacher's lesson? The latter situation might particularly apply when there is new learning for all teachers, and no individuals within the team feel confident enough with the content to teach without support. In this case, an instructional coach or resource teacher might teach the lesson, by herself, or co-plan and/or co-teach with the host teacher, amplifying the learning and social capital for all involved.

A final but critical question for those leading your effort to create collegial visits is: *Should administrators be a part of the collegial visits team?* There is no easy answer here. The terribly political answer I will offer is: *It depends*. Administrators who attend collegial visits alongside their school's teachers are able to (a) learn what the teachers are learning; (b) model for teachers the importance of learning; and (c) model for students that learning is important for everyone in the building, including their principal. Administrators can participate in visits if they have lived and supported the three foundational principles (empowerment, collegiality, and risk taking) to create an atmosphere of collaboration and trust. Further, administrators can never use these visits for anything other than their intended purpose—*professional learning*. In other words, if a teacher misspeaks while hosting a visit in her classroom, her principal cannot write about the mistake in the teacher's next informal observation. These visits are simply not about evaluation, and formal leaders need to consistently reinforce this message in the small moments during and surrounding each visit.

In my work with schools to implement collegial visits, some teams of teacher leaders have elected to leave their formal leaders out of the visits. The administrators provided their blessing and material support, through scheduling, coverage arrangements, and communication to staff members, but the formal leaders did not participate in the visits directly. In other settings, the administrators participated successfully as equal members of the visiting team. The climate within your school and the level of trust between teachers and administration will be important factors in the decision to include or exclude administrators from the visits. A compromise could involve leaving out administrators at first, bringing them into the visits later, once the practice is more established. Only you know your school's situation and context, so this decision is for your team alone.

## Creating Guiding Questions

In order to maintain the emphasis on the chosen focus, help visiting teachers attend to relevant components of this chosen focus, and provide structure for the debriefing session after the visit, I strongly recommend the creation of guiding questions for use by teachers as they take notes during the visit. Again, these questions are best written collaboratively, and, yet again, your team devoted to professional learning needs in your school is a logical group to undertake this task. These questions can be focused on the connection of the lesson to standards and/or why the host teacher made specific pedagogical decisions. The questions can also require visiting teachers to collect evidence as they view the host teacher's instruction. The questions can also serve as a call to action for visiting teachers about what they have seen and how their learning will affect teaching practice in their own classrooms. A sample set of guiding questions can be found in Figure 3.3, and a subset of these same sample questions, focused on visiting teachers' observations and reflections and displayed on a note-taking template, can be found in Figure 3.4. An editable and printable version of the note-taking template can be found in the eResources collection for this book.

As manifested in the samples shown in Figures 3.3 and 3.4, the sets of guiding questions need not be lengthy nor complicated. They simply need to provide teachers with purpose when observing and discussing the visit in the debriefing session. The guiding questions serve a purpose similar to anticipation guides used to prime students' brains for the content they will be reading. These guiding questions will be discussed again below in the section about debriefing sessions. First, we need to consider the logistics of the visits.

---

What curricular standard(s) did this lesson address?

At what point in the unit of study's sequence does this lesson fit?

What factors influenced your choices of materials, content, pedagogy, etc.? (i.e.: Why are you teaching this lesson the way you are today?)

What evidence illustrates the trajectory of learning for students prior to and after this lesson?

How has the focus strategy been implemented during the lesson?

What evidence did you observe of students using the taught strategy in question?

Reflect on how what you observed today can influence your practice in your classroom.

---

*Figure 3.3* Sample set of generalizable guiding questions for a round of collegial visits.

The Power of "Seeing It"

| Note-Taking Template for Collegial Visits ||
|---|---|
| Focus: _____ | Date: _____ |
| What evidence illustrates the trajectory of learning for students prior to and after this lesson? | How has the focus strategy been implemented during the lesson? |
| What evidence did you observe of students using the taught strategy in question? | Reflect on how what you observed today can influence your practice in your classroom. |
| Other Notes: ||

*Figure 3.4* Sample note-taking template for collegial visits with an unspecified focus.

## Creating the Space for Collegial Visits

You are likely asking yourself: *Self, this all sounds great, but how can we be physically present in the same classroom at the same time? We are all teaching!* This is a logical inquiry, and the answer is, again: *it depends*. A most obvious potential roadblock for many of the best ideas in education is time. There is so darn little of it during the teaching day. Thus, leaders need to be creative about allocating time for what is important. In the case of collegial visits, you will need to arrange for all the visiting teachers to be available at the same time to view the instruction of the host teacher, and then you will also need to find coverage for the host teacher, so she can join the debriefing session after the visit has ended.

There are multiple ways to provide coverage for collegial visits. However, the context of your school, as well as your district policies and protocols, will dictate what will work for you. For example, if you are fortunate enough to work in a school setting where substitute teachers are reliable and regularly available, you could simply book the number of substitute teachers you need to cover for the individuals listed above, and you are done. You could also maximize substitute usage by situating visits across grade levels or departments consecutively within one school day, so that the substitute teachers will simply rotate to the next collegial visit team when the first one is done. An example of this rotational model can be found in the sample collegial visits memo in Figure 3.5.

Of course, you might not be fortunate enough to work in an environment where substitute teachers are an option. If this is the case, I have seen schools rely on an internal system of teachers covering for each other's classrooms. It is also possible, when coverage situations are dire, to have the host teacher videotape the lesson for viewing by the "visiting" team later, such as during a professional learning community meeting. However, know that this videotaped method, while coverage problems are eliminated, does result in a "visit" that loses some of its luster. There is something to be said for being there, in the room where it happens, so to speak, and seeing the interactions among the classroom's members at the ground level. Video can never quite capture the nuance of live instruction. Nevertheless, when given the choice of working from a videotaped lesson or not having teachers learning from viewing each other's instruction, I will take the former 20 times out of 10, if there is such a thing!

The sample memo in Figure 3.5 also demonstrates some important messages for teachers about the visits. First, there is specific language about the focus of the visits and explicitly how this focus connects to the school improvement plan. It is important to make these connections to goals and other professional learning opportunities, when possible, to build a continuous through line of coherent work, which is consistent with our study of connected systems and teams in Chapter 2. Second, teachers are reminded that the visits represent new learning for everyone, including the host teachers, so it is important to

The Power of "Seeing It"

| | | |
|---|---|---|
| DATE: | October 15 | |
| TO: | All Staff | |
| FROM: | Jeremy Visone | |
| SUBJECT: | **<u>First Round of Collegial Visits</u>** | |

On **Tuesday, November 10**, we will have our first opportunity of the year to work as a grade level to view instruction by a colleague. As we have done in the past, substitutes will be secured to cover for the teachers involved. We will debrief immediately after each visit. NAME will be coordinating the coverage. We are breaking the hour (55 minutes, technically speaking) into two distinct blocks. First, the visit will take about 25 minutes. For the rest of the time, about 30 minutes, we will debrief in the conference room. Please bring to the visit something to write with, the debriefing questions, and a notebook or paper to jot down some informal notes.

Again, we have a focus for our visit. Following our work with NAME about Question Formulation Technique (QFT) and consistent with a specific action step in our School Improvement Plan (Goal #1: our academic goal) about our continued emphasis on questioning and discussion techniques, the focus of our visit will be *QFT*. You will observe either NAME or NAME and a colleague co-teaching the lesson. As always, we are extending ourselves to try something new, so we all should keep this in mind.

Here is the schedule of coverage times and lessons:

| | | |
|---|---|---|
| **Grade 4** | 9:00-9:25 | visit (all covered but HOST TEACHER NAME) |
| | 9:25-9:55 | debriefing (all covered) |
| **Grade K** | 10:00-10:25 | visit (all covered but HOST TEACHER NAME) |
| | 10:25-10:55 | **debriefing (all covered)** |
| **Grade 2** | 11:00-11:25 | visit (all covered but HOST TEACHER NAME) |
| | 11:25-11:55 | debriefing (all covered) |
| **Subs' Lunch** | 12:00-12:50 | |
| **Grade 3** | 1:00-1:25 | visit (all covered but HOST TEACHER NAME) |
| | 1:25-1:55 | debriefing (all covered) |
| **Grade 1** | 2:00-2:25 | visit (all covered but HOST TEACHER NAME) |
| | 2:25-2:55 | debriefing (all covered) |

Please let me know if you have any questions.

*Note.* All educator names were redacted and replaced with the word NAME.

*Figure 3.5* Sample collegial visits memo with rotating coverage model.

hold them to a realistic standard of expectation. The hosts are not necessarily experts. More accurately, they were often just the ones willing to try something new to afford the group a starting point for discussion and learning. Recall the importance of risk taking from our three foundational principles.

## Facilitating the Visit: Immersing Teachers in the Work

Instruct visiting team members to meet in the hallway a few minutes prior to the designated start time of the visit, assuming you have arranged coverage to relieve them from their own classrooms with time to do so. They should arrive with a hard surface on which to write (i.e. clipboard, book, padfolio, etc.), a printed set of the guiding questions or note-taking template with the same questions, and a writing utensil. Alternatively, if it is not too burdensome, the entire process could be electronic, with teachers wielding laptops or tablets. Participants should disrupt the lesson as little as five to eight adults possibly can. Start by assuming a position in the back/side of the classroom to allow the lesson to begin, but, once the lesson transitions to students working, model for the visiting team members how to quietly circulate around the room, noticing what students are doing and taking brief notes to serve as reminders later about what was observed. Also, model crouching down/leaning in next to students during their independent or group work time to inquire about what they are doing. These active means of participation will yield exponentially more learning fruit than the passive, leaning-on-the-back-counter approach. The visit can be as lengthy as you allow them to be within the confines of your schedule, but I have found that anywhere between 15 and 30 minutes can yield ample, meaningful learning, without taxing coverage systems too terribly. This time guideline gives the visiting team enough time to observe a lesson with some, if not all, of its key components (i.e. initiation, guided practice, independent practice, closure, etc.).

## Facilitating the Debriefing Session: Where Learning Connections Are Made

Likely, your teachers have left their visit with some inspiration, though they often have questions. The debriefing session, a distinctive feature of collegial visits, when compared to other models for common viewing of instruction (i.e. instructional rounds or walkthroughs), is purposeful in its inclusion of the *host teacher*, who needs both to hear much affirmation, gratitude, and general feedback from the visiting team and to answer the team's many questions. Any team working to implement collegial visits can devise its own protocol for debriefing sessions, but I will share a simple protocol that has worked well across different school levels and settings.

First, the facilitator models providing the host teacher with affirmation about aspects of the lesson that were especially noteworthy, as well as gratitude for the host teacher ... well ... *hosting* her colleagues. Then the facilitator provides each visiting team member a quick opportunity to similarly share some praise and gratitude. Recall the discussion earlier about keeping the process positive and emphasizing early wins to build buy in. The gratitude and affirmation of this first phase help to set this tone. The next phase of the meeting has the least defined parameters. Here, the conversation might evolve organically, which is my personal preference, or the facilitator can consult the guiding questions list to inquire answers from the visiting team or, when applicable, the host teacher. Finally, it is important to conclude the debriefing session with an inquiry to each visiting team member about her next step. Will the teachers experiment with some aspects of what they saw? Will they conduct some research on their own? Is there some prerequisite work teachers need in order to prepare their students for the type of lesson they observed during the visit? In short, each member of the team will have a concrete agenda item to push her to the next level. For a concise protocol for facilitating debriefing meetings, please see Figure 3.6.

## Summary

One significant way schools can manifest the three guiding principles of empowerment, collegiality, and risk taking is through the implementation of *collegial visits*, which are a structured protocol for peer observation. The traditional isolation of the teaching profession, combined with schedules that are jam-packed with student interactions and responsibilities, leaves teachers with little time to observe each other's instruction. Thus, it is incumbent upon leadership teams to provide opportunities for teachers to learn from one another, leveraging the power of social learning theory, social capital,

## The Power of "Seeing It"

**Protocol for Post-Collegial Visit Debriefing Meetings**

**Gratitude and Affirmation for Host Teacher:**
- facilitator **thanks the host teacher** for risk taking and willingness to share her classroom and learning with the team
- facilitator models for the team an **affirmation of at least one aspect of the viewed lesson** that was particularly noteworthy (i.e. exemplary in execution, effective with student learning, innovative, new learning, connected to a district or school priority, etc.)
- in a quick whip around, **each team member follows the lead of the facilitator** to provide the host teacher with gratitude and affirmation

**Discussion:**
- facilitator can allow **organic conversations** focused on the viewed lesson and learning for the team; guiding questions can be interjected when appropriate or if the organic conversation naturally pauses
- alternatively, facilitator asks the team/host teacher the **guiding questions** to generate a whole-team discussion; any team members can respond, or, if time allows, the facilitator could pose questions and whip around to each team member for a brief response

**Learning Outcomes and Next Steps:**
- facilitator asks each team member for **one take away** from the collegial visit, as well as a concrete **next step** to apply this learning in her classroom; a whip around works well here

**Sample Language for Facilitation:**
- *Thank you all for participating in this collegial visit about <focus>. Also, I would like to thank <host teacher> for her willingness to take a risk to try <focus instructional strategy> and open her classroom, so we can all learn from her experiences.*
- *I would like to highlight the connection between what <host teacher> showed us and our school improvement goal about <goal focus>. This is what we have been discussing at our professional learning workshops. <Host teacher> has helped us to see this in action.*
- *Of course, we never expect our hosts to be experts at the new strategy, but <host teacher> did an exceptional job with <aspect of the lesson>. It was evident by the <student observable outcome or behavior> that the students were really internalizing <purpose of lesson>.*
- *Our first guiding question is for <host teacher>. How did you arrive at this lesson? What were the lessons that preceded it, in terms of student skills? Tell us a little about your planning for this lesson.*
- *Now, I would like for each of you to quickly share one take away from today's lesson, including a concrete next step you will undertake to apply your learning from today.*

**Sample Language for Visiting Team Member Contributions:**
- *I really liked how you structured your <aspect of lesson>. That was effective at <student outcome or behavior>.*
- *I wonder about where you will go next with this topic. How will tomorrow's lesson look?*
- *I really appreciate seeing this live. You have given me a lot to think about with respect to <focus>. For example, I often struggle with <aspect of lesson>, and you had handled this very effectively.*

*Figure 3.6* Protocol for collegial visit debriefing meetings with sample language.

and decisional capital. Once established, these visits can be a gateway to increased collegial trust, sharing, and success.

In order to provide teachers the opportunity to view each other's instruction, leaders need to determine foci for the visits (preferably in collaboration with their professional learning team), assemble a strategic visiting team to participate, create guiding questions (preferably in collaboration with their professional learning team), create a schedule so that teachers are available at the same time, and facilitate the visits and debriefing sessions.

## Questions to Consider for Chapter 3:
### *The Power of "Seeing It": The Collegial Visit*

1. Think about the culture and climate of your school. Perhaps reference the empowerment, collegiality, and risk taking screener (Figure 1.2) from Chapter 1. How would you assess your school's readiness for teachers viewing each other's instruction for the purpose of professional learning?
2. Have teachers in your school seen colleagues teach? If they have, how has this practice been structured? If you have done so in the past, what did you gain from this experience? What worked in the past? What didn't?
3. What are the potential cultural roadblocks (i.e. fixed mindsets/dispositions, lack of buy in, lack of trust, etc.) to creating a system of teachers commonly viewing instruction of colleagues? What would be logical, proactive responses to those roadblocks?
4. What are the potential logistical roadblocks (i.e. scheduling, coverage, teaming, etc.) to creating a system of teachers commonly viewing instruction of colleagues? What would be logical, proactive responses to those roadblocks?
5. What are your own take aways from this chapter? What is a tangible next step for you and your school toward this ideal of collegial learning and sharing?
6. *What are you waiting for?* (This one is *rhetorical* …)

# References

Bambrick-Santoyo, P. (2019). If you want them to get it, get them to see it. *Educational Leadership, 76*(6), 18–22. https://eds-a-ebscohost-com.ccsu.idm.oclc.org/ehost/pdfviewer/pdfviewer?vid=1&sid=32ad7ae2-dc7a-4b0e-a275-07a84d1c4c55%40sdc-v-sessmgr03

Bandura, A. (1977). Self-efficacy: Toward a unifying theory of behavioral change. *Psychological Review, 84*(2), 191–215. https://doi.org/10.1037//0033-295X.84.2.191Self-efficacy

Bandura, A. (1986). *Social foundations of thought and action: A social cognitive theory*. Prentice-Hall.

Bandura, A. (1997). *Self-efficacy: The exercise of control*. W.H. Freeman & Company.

Baumert, J., Kunter, M., Blum, W., Brunner, M., Voss, T., Jordan, A., Klusmann, U., Krauss, S., Neubrand, M., & Tsai, Y.-M. (2010). Teachers' mathematical knowledge, cognitive activation in the classroom, and student progress. *American Educational Research Journal, 47*(1), 133–180. https://doi.org/10.3102/0002831209345157

Boudett, K. P., & Moody, L. (2013). Organizing for collaborative work. In K. P. Boudett, E. A. City, & R. J. Murnane (Eds.), *Data wise: A step-by-step guide to using assessment results to improve teaching and learning* (Rev. ed., pp. 13–34). Harvard Education Press.

City, E. A., Elmore, R. F., Fiarman, S. E., & Teitel, L. (2009). *Instructional rounds in education: A network approach to improving teaching and learning* (6th ed.). Harvard Education Press.

City, E. A., Kagle, M., & Teoh, M. B. (2005). Examining instruction. In K. P. Boudett, E. A. City, & R. J. Murnane (Eds.), *Data wise: A step-by-step guide to using assessment results to improve teaching and learning* (pp. 97–115). Harvard Education Press.

Croft, A., Coggshall, J. G., Dolan, M., Powers, E., & Killion, J. (2010). *Job-embedded professional development: What it is, who is responsible, and how to get it done well* [Issue Brief]. https://learningforward.org/wp-content/uploads/2017/08/job-embedded-professional-development.pdf

DeWitt, P. M. (2017). *Collaborative leadership: 6 influences that matter most*. Corwin Press.

Donaldson, M. L. (2016). Teacher evaluation reform: Focus, feedback, and fear. *Educational Leadership, 73*(8), 72–76.

DuFour, R., DuFour, R., Eaker, R., & Many, T. (2010). *Learning by doing: A handbook for professional learning communities at work* (2nd ed.). Solution Tree Press.

DuFour, R., & Eaker, R. (1998). *Professional learning communities at work: Best practices for enhancing student achievement.* Solution Tree Press.

DuFour, R., & Marzano, R. J. (2011). *Leaders of learning: How district, school, and classroom leaders improve student achievement.* Solution Tree Press.

Eaker, R., & Keating, J. (2012). *Every school, every team, every classroom: District leadership for growing professional learning communities at work.* Solution Tree Press.

Elmore, R. F. (2000). *Building a new structure for school leadership.* http://www.shankerinstitute.org/resource/building-new-structure-school-leadership

Elmore, R. F. (2005). *School reform from the inside out: Policy, practice, and performance.* Harvard Education Press.

Fullan, M. (2007). *The NEW meaning of educational change* (4th ed.). Teachers College Press.

Fullan, M., & Kirtman, L. (2019). *Coherent school leadership: Forging clarity from complexity.* ASCD.

Garet, M. S., Porter, A. C., Desimone, L., Birman, B. F., & Yoon, K. S. (2001). What makes professional development effective? Results from a national sample of teachers. *American Educational Research Journal, 38*, 915–945. https://doi.org/10.3102/00028312038004915

Guskey, T. R., & Passaro, P. D. (1994). Teacher efficacy: A study of construct dimensions. *American Educational Research Journal, 31*, 627–643. https://doi.org/10.3102/00028312031003627

Hargreaves, A., & Fullan, M. (2012). *Professional capital: Transforming teaching in every school.* Teachers College Press.

Hargreaves, A., & Fullan, M. (2013). The power of professional capital: With an investment in collaboration, teachers become nation builders. *Journal of Staff Development, 34*(3), 36–39.

Hargreaves, A., & O'Connor, M. T. (2018). *Collaborative professionalism: When teaching together means learning for all.* Corwin.

Hoerr, T. R. (2016). What's important: We must focus on what's truly important--not just what's urgent. *Educational Leadership, 74*(4), 90–91.

Johnston, W. R., & Tsai, T. (2018). *The prevalence of collaboration among American teachers: National findings from the American teacher panel.* https://pdfs.semanticscholar.org/9178/4e7923c2b8419d6ab4f2b2628c217c46de57.pdf

Jung, L. A., Frey, N., Fisher, D., & Kroener, J. (2019). *Your students, my students, our students: Rethinking equitable and inclusive classrooms.* ASCD.

Kaufman, T. E. (2007). Examining instruction: Murphy K-8 School unlocks the classroom. In K. P. Boudett & J. L. Steele (Eds.), *Data wise in action: Stories of schools using data to improve teaching and learning* (pp. 87–104). Harvard Education Press.

Klassen, R. M., Tze, V. M. C., Betts, S. M., & Gordon, K. A. (2011). Teacher efficacy research 1998–2009: Signs of progress or unfulfilled promise? *Educational Psychology Review, 23*(1), 21–43. https://doi.org/10.1007/sl0648-010-9141-8

Leana, C. R. (2011). The missing link in school reform. *Stanford Social Innovation Review, 9*(4), 30–35.

Learning Forward. (2017). *Standards for professional learning.* https://learningforward.org/standards-for-professional-learning

Liu, Y., Visone, J., Mongillo, M. B., & Lisi, P. (2019). What matters to teachers if evaluation is meant to help them improve? *Studies in Educational Evaluation, 61,* 41–54. https://doi.org/10.1016/j.stueduc.2019.01.006

National Archives and Records Administration. (2009). Department of Education, State Fiscal Stabilization Fund program: Final rule. *Federal Register, 74*(217), 58436–58525. https://www.gpo.gov/fdsys/pkg/FR-2009-11-12/pdf/E9-27161.pdf

Organisation for Economic Co-operation and Development. (n.d.). *About.* Retrieved September 13, 2021, from https://www.oecd.org/about/

Penuel, W. R., Fishman, B. J., Yamaguchi, R., & Gallagher, L. P. (2007). What makes professional development effective? Strategies that foster curriculum implementation. *American Educational Research Journal, 44*(4), 921–958. https://doi.org/10.3102/0002831207308221

Reeves, D. B. (2009). *Leading change in your school: How to conquer myths, build commitment, and get results.* ASCD.

Reeves, P. M., Pun, W. H., & Chung, K. S. (2017). Influence of teacher collaboration on job satisfaction and student achievement. *Teaching and Teacher Education, 67,* 227–236. https://doi.org/10.1016/j.tate.2017.06.016

Ronka, D. P. (2007). Organizing for collaborative work: Pond Cove Elementary School lays the groundwork. In K. P. Boudett & J. L. Steele (Eds.), *Data wise in action: Stories of schools using data to improve teaching and learning* (pp. 11–28). Harvard Education Press.

Ross, J. A. (2013). Teacher efficacy. In J. Hattie & E. M. Anderman (Eds.), *International guide to student achievement* (pp. 266–267). Routledge.

Schleicher, A. (2016). *Teaching excellence through professional learning and policy reform: Lessons from around the world.* OECD Publishing, Paris. https://doi.org/10.1787/9789264252059-en

Senge, P. M. (1990). *The fifth discipline: The art and practice of the learning organization.* Doubleday/Currency.

Sterrett, W. (2015). *Igniting teacher leadership: How do I empower my teachers to lead and learn.* ASCD.

Stinson, S. (2017). *Learning designs.* Learning Forward Standards. https://learningforward.org/standards/learning-designs/shirnetha-stinson

Tekkumru-Kisa, M., Stein, M. K., & Coker, R. (2018). Teachers' learning to facilitate high-level student thinking: Impact of a video-based professional development. *Journal of Research in Science Teaching, 55,* 479–502. https://doi.org/10.1002/tea.21427

Tschannen-Moran, M., Hoy, A. W., & Hoy, W. K. (1998). Teacher efficacy: Its meaning and measure. *Review of Educational Research, 68,* 202–248. https://journals-sagepub-com.ccsu.idm.oclc.org/doi/pdf/10.3102/00346543068002202

Visone, J. D. (2016). A learning community of colleagues enhancing practice. *Kappa Delta Pi Record, 52*(2), 66–70. https://doi.org/10.1080/00228958.2016.1156511

Visone, J. D. (2018). Developing social and decisional capital in US National Blue Ribbon Schools. *Improving Schools, 21*(2), 158–172. https://doi.org/10.1177/1365480218755171

Visone, J. D. (2019). What teachers never have time to do: Peer observation as professional learning. *Professional Development in Education,* 1–15. https://doi.org/10.1080/19415257.2019.1694054

Visone, J. D. (2020). Pre-launch preparations for a peer observation initiative viewed through a concerns model. *Professional Development in Education*, *46*, 130–144. https://doi.org/10.1080/19415257.2019.1585385

Vygotsky, L. S. (1978). *Mind in society*. Harvard University Press.

Wei, R. C., Darling-Hammond, L., & Adamson, F. (2010). *Professional development in the United States: Trends and challenges*.

# Building a Teacher Leadership System

As the newly appointed principal of Ruth Bader Ginsberg Elementary School (RBG), Tiana was hoping to build off the school's past practices. She engaged in a listening campaign during the first few months after her appointment, aiming to determine how her predecessor, Malcolm, had run the school.

"I am sorry that I don't have much to share," offered Laverne, the widely regarded strongest teacher in the school. Her students regularly posted the top scores, and parents had already started contacting Tiana to plead for their children's placement in Laverne's classroom. Tiana had specifically asked Laverne about how the process for student placement worked, amid a larger informal interview about school operations, in general. "You know, we all put in our requests and hope for the best. Malcolm would take all that information and get back to us with the lists."

"Alright, Laverne. Thanks for that. Let's shift to something else. How about professional learning? What does that look like here at RBG?" Tiana pivoted.

"Well, we have a few days that the district has set aside for PD, and we have one day each month where the kids go home early, so we can have PD in the afternoon for two hours—" Laverne began.

"I'm sorry," Tiana interjected, "I am not looking for the structure; I am wondering how the focus of professional learning is determined and who facilitates it."

"Oh, I see," Laverne responded, apologetically. "I have no idea where the topics come from—central office, maybe?—and Malcolm or someone from central office would lead the PDs. Sometimes, they would hire somebody from outside the district."

"Thanks for your help, Laverne," Tiana remarked, understanding that there was much more that she needed to learn.

DOI: 10.4324/9781003190370-4

Later that week, Tiana sent her teachers an electronic survey to collect data about committee and team membership. She indicated that she was seeking volunteers for committees about school improvement planning, school safety, professional learning, and more. After the deadline of two weeks' time had passed, Tiana scanned the results, disappointed. Less than 20 of her 40 teachers had volunteered, and most committees and teams had fewer than three volunteers.

What is going on here? Tiana wondered.

Tiana also spent a good portion of her first three months on the job hiring new staff. Of her 40 teaching positions, she had to fill five of them immediately upon her appointment, and she came to learn that seven more teachers were hired the year before. This fact would not be so surprising with an aging teacher population, except for the fact that the building only had two retirements in the last year. Most of the teachers leaving were doing so by resigning to take positions in other districts. Though she could not ask these teachers, herself, as they had departed prior to the inception of her tenure, she asked administrators in the personnel office to share exit survey data from these teachers. What these surveys revealed was telling:

"I never had any opportunity for growth. I felt stifled there," remarked one teacher, who subsequently took a job teaching the same grade level as she had at RBG.

"I did not feel supported." remarked another teacher, who left after only her third year in the building. She, too, settled into a job teaching the same grade level in a neighboring district. Other teachers' remarks echoed these. None of the exit interview transcripts mentioned money or student concerns. Tiana was aware that lack of administrative support was a major factor in teachers leaving their schools.

Tiana began to have second thoughts about accepting her position. What was wrong with RBG that teachers were leaving?

Seeking a reason for optimism about her new school, Tiana frequently engaged her teachers in conversations about teaching and learning. To Tiana, this was always an uplifting topic. One day, she asked Jonnelle, an enthusiastic fourth-year teacher, "Tell me about what your Grade 3 team is doing for this upcoming curricular unit about fractions."

Jonnelle, unsure of the inquiry's aim, replied, "I can't really speak to what the others are doing, but I will be …"

Many factors likely contributed to the situation at RBG. While there was no evidence presented indicating this school's professionals were outwardly negative toward one another, collegiality, one of this book's guiding principles, is certainly not ideally operationalized. Teachers were unaware of how the school operates, and they did not know what each other were teaching. Further, formal leaders seemed to make all the decisions, including about student placement and professional learning. When teachers needed to know something, they had been conditioned to seek this information from formal leaders. You have probably figured out that one important element missing from this school's operation is *teacher leadership*.

But, Jeremy, *you might be asking yourself, why do teachers need to be leaders? That's why administrators get paid the "big bucks"!* I am so glad you asked. We examine the case for teacher leadership next.

## Why Your School Needs Teacher Leadership

Let's begin with the obvious. The work of leading a school is simply too complex, too dynamic, and—let's be honest—*too much* for one individual (or small group of individuals) with a formal leadership title to effectively manage all the needs (Danielson, 2007; Nerlino, 2020). A principal or assistant principal cannot be in all meetings or deal with all situations as they arise. It is important to have teacher leaders providing "coverage" and stability for the many leadership vacuums created by the impossibly busy schedules of formal leaders. According to Harris and Jones (2019):

> The possibility and potential of teacher leadership remains a central issue within the international discourse about educational reform and change. This potential is reflected in a range of contemporary publications that forcefully argue that teachers should play a far more central role in decision making and policy formation.
>
> (p. 123)

This very book can be added to the list as one such "contemporary publication"!

It is important to distinguish that teacher leaders do not need to have formal titles. As concluded by Wenner and Campbell (2017), in their extensive review on the topic, teacher leaders are those educators with primary teaching responsibilities, who also accept leadership roles outside of their classrooms. In a response to Wenner and Campbell's review, Nguyen et al. (2020) agreed that most definitions offered in the literature for teacher leadership involved teachers working beyond their typical classroom duties, but these teacher leaders were more influencers than they were individuals with formal roles or titles. Teacher leaders are those teachers whose influence extends beyond the students in their own classrooms. Their actions affect students who are not "theirs," families of students who are not "theirs," colleagues, and formal leaders.

Upon returning to our three guiding principles, teacher leadership is logically connected to all three. In case you were most distracted during the first three chapters, or you are beginning your study of this book in Chapter 4, these principles are:

(a) **empowerment**: Our staff members feel competent and believe that they are equipped to make decisions in the best interest of our students and school. Our teachers have sound ideas that can improve what we do;
(b) **collegiality**: Our staff works together to solve problems of practice. We do not work in isolation. What we learn, we share; and
(c) **risk taking**: We do not advance if we do not try new things and experiment. We are not afraid to do things differently.

The three foundational principles are displayed again in Figure 4.1.

Empowerment is the simplest connection to teacher leadership, and there is a "chicken or the egg" reciprocal relationship between the two. As you will learn in this chapter, teacher leadership is accentuated when teachers are empowered to be leaders (Nguyen et al., 2020). In the reverse

| | |
|---|---|
| **empowerment** | Our staff members feel competent and believe that they are equipped to make decisions in the best interest of our students and school. Our teachers have sound ideas that can improve what we do. |
| **collegiality** | Our staff works together to solve problems of practice. We do not work in isolation. What we learn, we share. |
| **risk taking** | We do not advance if we do not try new things and experiment. We are not afraid to do things differently. |

*Figure 4.1* The three foundational principles to empower teacher leadership.

direction, teachers who engage in teacher leadership work are empowered by their increased impact and improved skillsets (Visone, 2018, 2020). Thus, there is a positive reinforcement loop between empowerment and teacher leadership. As articulated well by Nerlino (2020), "Being able to exercise agency improves teachers' sense of efficacy" (p. 119). In other words, having some control over your circumstances can improve your belief that you can make a difference.

Collegiality is also connected to teacher leadership, as the former serves as an important prerequisite condition for the latter (Nguyen et al., 2020). Many teacher leader behaviors and dispositions can be described, globally, as collegial. For example, teachers who mentor less-experienced colleagues; share lesson plans and resources with colleagues; or open their classrooms to their colleagues for collegial visits, which were outlined as a peer-observation vehicle for professional learning in Chapter 3, are acting as leaders via their collegiality. Not surprisingly, research has shown that student achievement is greater in schools where teachers collaborate more (Johnson, 2019).

Finally, risk taking can be nurtured by teacher leaders, through the aforementioned collegial behaviors. When teacher leaders model for their less-confident colleagues how to try a new strategy during a collegial visit, as we examined in Chapter 3, these teacher leaders foster a culture of support for risk taking, as well as push professional learning to a more dynamic and, frankly, effective place (Nerlino, 2020).

The presence of teacher leaders in a school contributes to what is known as a *distributed leadership* model (Diamond & Spillane, 2016; Leithwood et al., 2007; Nerlino, 2020; Spillane, 2006; Spillane et al., 2001), whereby leadership does not simply reside within a few formal leaders with administrative roles. Rather, the leadership of the school is spread across many roles and individuals at different levels of the organization, and this approach, again not surprisingly, has been associated with school improvement (Hairon & Goh, 2015; Teacher Leadership Exploratory Consortium, 2012) and increased teacher job satisfaction (Torres, 2018). This distributed approach is important, since the inability of formal leaders to meet all the leadership needs of their schools, as identified above by Danielson (2007) and Nerlino (2020), can limit the impact of leadership, which giants in our field have identified as a quintessentially important school-related factor that influences student achievement. Leadership is second in its influence on student achievement only to ... *duh!* ... teaching (Leithwood et al., 2004).

According to an influential group of educators across many different organizations (i.e. preK–12 school districts, universities, teacher unions, state-level educational agencies, school administrator associations, etc.) known as the Teacher Leadership Exploratory Consortium (2012), teacher leadership maximizes principal effectiveness. Thus, spreading leadership practice among many individuals is both a matter of survival for formal leaders and a means to impact student learning in a profound way.

Further, to extend the idea of distributed leadership enhancing job satisfaction for teachers, recent authors (Berg & Zoellick, 2019; Nerlino, 2020) have suggested that teacher leadership is an attraction for teachers to remain engaged and interested in the teaching profession, which can be flat in nature (Read: *Teachers like it! Teacher leadership opportunities can influence teachers to want to stay in their schools!*). Specifically, teachers have reported increases in motivation, pedagogical knowledge, self-efficacy, and commitment, among other positive, individual affective developments resulting from their leadership activities (Nguyen et al., 2020). Group-level factors discovered in the authors' review included increased collective efficacy, improved school culture, increased collaboration, and higher levels of group commitment. Not surprisingly, the authors found positive effects on student learning, resulting from teacher leadership influences over instructional practices and school climate.

These findings were directly and powerfully corroborated by a study that sought to determine the relationship between teacher leadership and student achievement (Shen et al., 2020). The authors, via a meta-analysis that statistically combined the results of 21 quantitative studies attempting to link teacher leadership and student achievement, found that there was a small, positive, statistically significant correlation ($r = .19$) between the two variables. For any readers despondent about the seemingly low value for the relationship, fret not! Compare this result to another, oft-cited meta-analysis (Marzano et al., 2005), which identified the statistically significant correlation of *principal* leadership with student achievement to be .25. Given that, as stated above, principal leadership has been identified *as second to only teaching* as an influence on student achievement (Leithwood et al., 2004), teacher leadership compares as quite a meaningful influence, after all, especially considering how many other factors are also impacting student achievement. Through examining different dimensions of teacher leadership and their individual effects on student achievement, Shen et al. (2020) determined that instructional leadership ($r = .21$) by teachers was the most highly correlated with increased student achievement of all dimensions (as opposed to making school-wide decisions, interacting with families, influencing school climate, or promoting professional learning, which all had correlations between .15 and .20).

In the unlikely event that you are not yet convinced, still another compelling argument for the importance of cultivating teacher leadership in your school is the fact that it is a consistent characteristic observed in effective, award-winning schools. In some of my own research about National Blue Ribbon Schools (Visone, 2020), I found that these highly effective schools—recognized for either their overall student achievement or exemplary gap-closing success—count teacher leadership as a factor in their unusually positive student outcomes. Specifically, I examined schools' applications to the National Blue Ribbon Schools Program, which are written by the schools' staff members, to determine if there was evidence of teacher leadership practice. The application prompts inquire about curricula, student support, school leadership, among other general topics. However, *the prompts do not mention teacher leadership, at all.* Thus, any espoused teacher leadership connections made by the school staff members were unsolicited. Despite the lack of direct questioning about teacher leadership, these highly successful schools repeatedly and consistently reported abundant teacher leadership practices. First and foremost, teachers were presented across all sampled applications as instructional leaders, exhibiting such behaviors as mentoring less-experienced teachers, sharing instructional resources with colleagues, updating curricula, and influencing and facilitating professional learning. None of these instructional leadership practices should be unexpected, since these educators are, of course, *teachers* first. Thus, focusing on instructional practice and then sharing their learning with others falls squarely in their professional wheelhouse, so to speak. Further, they have instructional expertise (especially since the COVID-19 pandemic began and remote learning became a widespread "thing" in preK–12 schools) that many administrators do not possess. Teacher leaders have valuable pedagogical perspectives to offer, but I'd bet you already knew that!

However, the influence of teacher leaders in National Blue Ribbon Schools was not limited to instructional leadership. These influential teachers also were decision makers, serving on and/or leading committees and teams, modeling communications to the school community, and participating in the hiring process for new teachers. Further, teacher leaders were identified as innovators of practice and advocates for the professional learning needs of staff. Finally, as a brief preview into the work of Chapter 5, these highly effective schools identified that their teachers were often leaders *beyond* their own schools, serving in positions of leadership on state and national education groups, sharing effective practices with other schools, and presenting at conferences. The success of National Blue Ribbon Schools was, in the staff members' own words, intertwined with the work of teacher leaders, displaying strong alignment with the distributed leadership model advocated in the literature (Diamond & Spillane, 2016; Leithwood et al., 2007; Nerlino, 2020; Spillane, 2006; Spillane et al., 2001). Teacher leadership is important to schools realizing the highest levels of student success, and improving student success is why we are all in this profession and likely why you are reading this text!

## Demystifying Leadership for Teachers

Typically, when I mention the concept of teacher leadership, I sense that teachers are not quite sure what the construct means. For some, they are picturing an actual, named quasi-leadership role, as is the case in some districts and schools. The role might actually be entitled "Teacher Leader," where teachers might supervise an intern, help administrators with formal curricular matters, sit on interview committees, and mentor new teachers. Other manifestations of this formal role concept for teachers could be team or departmental leaders, who earn a title for handling some administrative tasks. These formal, stipend-earning positions are certainly a manifestation of teacher leadership in some settings. Other teachers, when considering the meaning of teacher leadership, imagine a teacher who is seeking to become an administrator. Again, this is just one manifestation of teacher leadership. However, these examples do not represent the totality of the construct, and, as the first three chapters of this book have attested, are but a fraction of the subset of teachers who should be functioning as leaders in any school building. There is no need to envision teachers wearing a suffragette-style sash that says "Teacher Leader" or a giant letter "L" on their chests (for *leader*, not loser!); teacher leadership can and should be ubiquitous for maximized student success. If only formal leaders could convince their teachers that many of their existing behaviors are, in fact, teacher leadership.

Teachers are not the only ones who disagree about the meaning of the term "teacher leadership." Wenner and Campbell (2017), in their aforementioned, comprehensive review of literature about the construct of teacher leadership, agreed with a foundational study by York-Barr and Duke (2004) that, even after a decade more of scholarship and practitioner-based writing, teacher leadership was still not universally defined. Most recently, Berg and Zoellick (2019) concurred that the concept is not well-defined. To provide some consistency, they offered four dimensions that can help to frame conversations about teacher leadership. These dimensions are:

- **legitimacy**: which includes whether or not the designation of "teacher leader" is connected to a formal role (i.e. mentor teacher, data team leader, instructional coach, head teacher, etc.) and from where the leadership designation comes (i.e. colleagues telling a teacher that she is leader, a principal bestowing a title, teachers deciding to be a leader on their own, etc.);
- **support**: which considers how teachers' work as leaders is maintained (i.e. material support, scheduling, time, professional learning, etc.) and who provides the support (i.e. principals, colleagues, university partners, etc.);
- **objective**: which refers to the aim of teacher leadership work (i.e. instruction, school culture, policy, etc.) and what parties determine this aim (i.e. formal leaders, outside agency, higher education, teacher leaders themselves, etc.); and
- **method**: which explains how the teacher leader works to accomplish the objective (i.e. leading professional learning, communicating, coaching, inspiring, etc.) and from where the method of delivery emanates (i.e. formal leader, teacher leader, colleague, etc.).

This framework can be useful when classifying teacher leadership work. Keep these dimensions in mind, as we delve into the business of creating a supportive culture for teacher leadership. The present landscape in education provides a wide range of inclusiveness for aspiring teacher leaders. In short, if you want a seat at the teacher leadership table, there is room for you.

In my work with teacher leaders, one of my first goals is to demystify the concept of teacher leadership for them. I need to help them understand that their leadership is not magic, nor does it need to be formal (*not that there's anything wrong with formal leadership titles*, thinks the former principal!). My simple test for teachers is for them to figuratively turn around. If

# Building a Teacher Leadership System

others are following their lead, then they are leaders. Teachers can inherently be a humble group to a fault. So many teachers express to me that they do not know if what they have to offer will be viewed as valuable to others. Part of the work of teacher leadership development is confidence building. When leaders and peers provide messages to teachers that they have valuable information to share, often, they will. We will examine a more formal framework for supporting the work of teacher leaders later in this chapter, but, first, to help demystify leadership practices for teachers, I often pose reflective questions about their own actions. Figure 4.2 displays a list of potential teacher leadership inquiries. Naturally, affirmative answers to these questions would illustrate examples of teacher leadership.

These questions can be excellent conversation starters with a group of teachers to illustrate that so much of what they (likely) do already is teacher leadership. I imagine that, if you are a teacher reading this book, you had several to many "yes" responses. You are a teacher leader, already! For the formal leaders, you likely can picture the faces of specific teachers as you

---

Do you facilitate professional learning experiences for your colleagues?

Do you serve as a mentor or cooperating teacher for a beginning or aspiring teacher?

Have you assisted your administrator in making decisions related to school operations?

Have you served on a school-wide committee or team that makes decisions that impact the school?

Do you share resources, pedagogical ideas, and/or lessons with colleagues?

Have you coordinated any events for students at your grade, department, or school level?

Do you maintain an open mind, positive disposition, and growth mindset about new initiatives?

Do you bring new and innovative ideas to your team, grade level, or department?

Do you sometimes serve as the spokesperson for your team, grade level, or department?

Are you a colleague to whom others come for advice?

Do you work collaboratively with others to solve problems?

Would you consider yourself an "outside-the-box" thinker?

---

*Figure 4.2* Teacher leadership reflective questions.

answer each question. These are your teacher leaders, and they need your support and encouragement to maximize their influence and your collective success.

Another way to broach the subject of demystification is through literature. The influential educational thinker Charlotte Danielson wrote a concise and thought-provoking article in the periodical *Educational Leadership* that provides teachers with many concrete examples of teacher leadership in practice (Danielson, 2007). She offered some ideas about school-wide leadership actions that teachers could undertake. Examples included serving as the school-wide liaison for new teachers, helping to craft a new schedule, or leading a school-wide committee to examine homework usage by teachers. From an instructional leadership perspective, Danielson suggests mentoring activities, data-driven decision making, or leading a lesson study. For communication and community relations activities, she suggests creating a forum for teachers to discuss student data, publishing a departmental newsletter for parents, or initiating a system for core academic and other subject area teachers to speak interdepartmentally about student matters.

Another recent conceptualization of teacher leadership was outlined by Hairon and Goh (2015), who identified three teacher leadership dimensions as building a collegial and collaborative culture, promoting teacher development and learning, and enabling change in teachers' instructional practices, all of which would be considered part of the normal work of teachers. None of these suggestions above would likely seem to be too daunting to many teachers, so challenging "leadership" stereotypes for teachers can be helpful in moving toward distributed leadership ideals.

Finally, a very comprehensive and helpful self-assessment inventory is provided by the Center for Strengthening the Teaching Profession (2009). This inventory has five broad categories of focus: working with adult learners, collaborative work, communication, knowledge of content and pedagogy, and systems thinking. Potential teacher leaders can rate themselves in each category related to knowledge and skills, as well as dispositions. There are reflective prompts to allow teachers to construct meaning from the ratings and plan for their next steps. The uniform resource locator (aka URL, or, in plain English, web address) for this assessment tool can be found in the references list entry for this source at the end of this chapter. As with the frameworks listed above, this self-assessment allows potential teacher leaders to view much of their present work as leadership, building their confidence, while also providing them the inspiration to learn and do more with their newfound self-assuredness. If you are a teacher reading this book, how many of the actions mentioned in the first part of this chapter resonate with your own practice? If you are a formal leader reading this text, how many of your teachers serve in these capacities?

The awareness of teacher leadership accessibility is a positive first step for your school to maximize its potential. Now that we have demystified the concept, we will get more specific about teacher leadership expectations, followed by how teacher leadership can be nurtured and supported.

## Teacher Leadership by the Standards

Another notable attempt at framing the work of teacher leaders was undertaken by many prominent educational organizations (Teacher Leadership Exploratory Consortium, 2012). Rather than try to create an all-encompassing job description for teacher leaders, this consortium developed seven domains that outline the work of leadership, broadly. Within each domain, the authors shared examples of how teacher leaders could support this type of leadership work. For example, the first domain relates to creating a culture of collaboration that works to improve educator practice and advance student learning. One way teacher leaders can satisfy the spirit of this function operationally is to facilitate group work within their grade levels or departments to solve problems, make decisions, and promote change. The complete list of domains, which are known as the *Teacher Leader Model Standards*, can be found in Figure 4.3.

These standards outline teacher leadership behaviors and activities, rather than larger roles, though one can infer some of the roles mentioned earlier by other authors, such as mentor, professional development facilitator, and instructional leader. As with the frameworks shared earlier, they provide another lens and "idea bank," against which teachers can compare their present and aspirational efforts.

## Fostering Teacher Leadership Formally: *The Teacher Leadership Academy*

It cannot be overstated that a culture that supports teachers is critical to encourage their emergence as leaders (Crowther et al., 2009; Katzenmeyer

> fostering a **collaborative culture** to support educator development and student learning, which entails facilitation, collaboration, modeling, and inclusivity;
>
> accessing and using **research to improve practice and student learning**, which includes leading for data-driven decision making, seeking research-based practices, and collaborating with higher education to enhance practices;
>
> promoting **professional learning** for continuous improvement, which includes addressing teachers' professional learning needs through traditional and job-embedded means;
>
> **facilitating improvements in instruction and student learning**, which involves serving in mentoring roles, basing improvement feedback based upon observation of instruction, and leading improvement conversations with a focus on diversity and equity;
>
> promoting the **use of assessments** and data for school and district improvement, which entails leading the creation of assessments, helping teachers use a variety of assessments to make informed decisions on student progress, and having difficult conversations based upon student performance data;
>
> improving **outreach and collaboration** with families and community, which requires an understanding of and appreciation for diversity, leading to equitable school outcomes for all students;
>
> **advocating for student learning and the profession**, which is about sharing and giving voice to issues of import to educators outside the context of one's classroom or school.

*Figure 4.3* Summary of the Teacher Leader Model Standards.

& Moller, 2009; Nerlino, 2020), and the foundation created by adhering to the three guiding principles is a means to foster this type of culture. In some of my own research (Visone, 2018, 2020), teacher leaders consistently pointed to their formal leaders' support (or lack thereof, sadly) as intertwined with their degree of success in advancing leadership aims. Without leaders who empower, encourage collegiality, and allow for risk taking, teacher leadership is unlikely to take root, and it will certainly not be sustained, since teacher leadership occurs within a climate of collaboration and trust (Nguyen et al., 2020). This requirement for a supportive foundation is why Chapter 1 implored schools to examine their most basic relational qualities and professional habits. Without trusting relationships and within a rigid hierarchical structure, for example, who will want to raise her hand to be a leader among peers? In case you are thinking intently about this one, the answer is: *no one!*

Many authors have offered pathways to engender and support teacher leadership. Some have focused on university graduate programs that offered a course sequence and/or degree in teacher leadership (Ovington et al., 2002; Ross et al., 2011; Taylor et al., 2011). However, this model is costly and likely out of reach for most schools for widespread use.

One intriguing and informative model involves a unique collaboration between school districts, teacher unions, and higher education. Dr. Betty Sternberg, former Commissioner of Education for the State of Connecticut, directed the Teacher Leader Fellowship Program (TLFP) from Central Connecticut State University from 2016-2021, and she now operates the Teacher Leader Fellowship Academy at Sacred Heart University. In both versions of the program, participating preK–12 public school districts across Connecticut send a small team of teacher leaders and administrators to a series of professional learning experiences—often facilitated by some of the teacher leaders, themselves—throughout the year. The teacher leaders apply acquired leadership skills and confidence by facilitating leadership projects in their own schools and districts. The teachers are supported by their administrators, who are engaged in the work alongside the teachers. Each spring, the TLFP hosted an Annual Institute, open to all preK–12 educators in the state. At this one-day event, part conference and part celebration, along with well-known keynote speakers, the teacher leadership teams were part of the draw, as they led professional learning breakout sessions, often sharing their leadership learnings and projects with others from across the state. Other presenters, representing higher education, preK–12 districts not participating in the TLFP, and teacher unions also led breakout sessions. This event is an example of the type of collegial sharing beyond one's school that is the focus of Chapter 5.

Dr. Sternberg shared with me that, through membership in the TLFP, "People get to think in creative and innovative ways. [The TLFP] pushes them out of their silos into something that's joyful for them" (B. Sternberg, personal communication, January 27, 2021). Recall that, earlier in this chapter, I noted research has shown leadership opportunities for teachers can increase teacher's job satisfaction. Dr. Sternberg also noted that the TLFP validates for teachers that they can do more than just teach their own students. It broadens their perspective. So valuable is this program to its participants and their districts that, in spite of the COVID-19 pandemic upending the professional and personal lives of educators during 2020 and into 2021, many districts continued to participate in the program during the 2020–2021 school year. Consider that meetings took place from 4:30 to 6:00 PM, after these educators had endured full school days in masks, live with students, and/or in front of their computer screen, teaching remotely. Further, one district's teachers continued participating, *even after their superintendent* (who shall remain nameless!) *discontinued official district membership* out of concern for the teachers being overwhelmed! This willingness to participate in the face of unprecedented challenges speaks to the power and draw of teacher leadership opportunities.

I know that you might be wondering: *Jeremy, how are we supposed to operate a program of this scale at our school?* The short answer is: *You can't.* (Sorry.) However, there is so much to learn from this successful model that you *can* apply in your school. First, as mentioned earlier in this chapter, teachers' self-efficacy is improved when teachers have agency and perceive they have a say in decision making. Thus, providing teachers with a forum in your own school for expressing their leadership can be a powerful influence on their mindset. Further, this type of structure—professional learning, collaboration within a community of like-minded individuals, work alongside supportive administrators to lead projects of interest, etc.—can show teachers that they are *valued*. As discussed earlier in this chapter, teachers often humbly do not view themselves as leaders, and many believe that their ideas are not worthy of sharing. Formal leaders can help dispel this myth and provide teachers with the message and, by extension, confidence, that they can and should contribute.

Further, as a bonus, TLFP members told Dr. Sternberg that their participation helped them to be better teachers. In a parallel fashion, they returned to their schools and provided their own students with more choice and agency, teaching more democratically, thus paying the cycle of empowerment forward, resulting in increased student engagement and higher quality student work. This is a powerful rationale to empower teacher leadership at your school. Next, we examine how to apply our learning about engendering teacher leadership to your school.

Connected to the stated aim of this book of building teacher leadership at the school level, Sinha and Hanuscin (2017) studied how teachers could implement projects that would provide opportunities to display their leadership skills. Their model was within the structure of a school district. Throughout the teacher leaders' learning and project implementation, school administrators encouraged them, provided them with helpful feedback, recognized them for their efforts, and generally supported them with needed resources to successfully complete their projects. This model is consistent with some of my own research with teacher leadership academy work in schools (Visone, 2018, 2020). By providing teachers a dedicated space and forum for collaborative problem solving, professional learning, and explicit support for their projects, you can strategically engender teacher leadership. This is not the only way for teacher leadership to develop, but it is a purposeful method that is low cost and high yield. You can recruit a small, dedicated group of teachers to undertake a leadership journey, and this model (the Teacher Leadership Academy) will be outlined next.

## Who Should Participate?

I am not informed enough about your context to tell you who should participate in a potential Teacher Leadership Academy (TLA) at your school. However, I would recommend that you provide your staff with notions about the ideal candidates for your TLA. In this way, teachers will be able to identify with your desired characteristics and see themselves in your initiative. Only your team can determine how wide a net you wish to cast. However, there are some general decision points you will need to consider. First, will you want to include teachers with a specific experience level? You may wish to include only teachers with at least three to five years of teaching experience, so you are assured of minimum experience in the field prior to having them consider leadership. However, a disadvantage to this limitation is you might necessarily disqualify some truly gifted new teachers from participating when they arrived at your school ready to share and lead. Also, you might consider participants' own leadership preparation. Thus, you might want to disqualify teachers who have already undertaken leadership coursework to obtain their administrative certification, to avoid repetitive learning for these individuals. A disadvantage of this disqualification is that, again, you might miss the opportunity to empower some very skilled and knowledgeable teacher leaders. Further, the teachers with advanced coursework will have great perspectives and skills to share with their colleagues. In short, you will need to contemplate how to bound your group, considering the consequences of any limitations you place on its membership.

Your team will also need to consider how many TLA participants you wish to include. This decision is completely up to your team and can be influenced by several factors, including the number of available facilitators, size of your district/school, facilitators' experience and comfort level, and degree of administrative support, to name a few. Anywhere between 5 and 20 members provide for ample collegial sharing, while keeping the group nimble enough that all feel heard, and facilitators can provide participants with the individual attention they need.

Another consideration for your team is role. A TLA does not need to be limited to teachers. I can hear you whispering to yourself: *But, Jeremy, "teacher" is the first word!* This is certainly true, and it is likely that most participants in the teacher leadership activity I have outlined in this chapter and entire book will be teachers. However, there are plenty of other roles in schools that can contribute a great deal to the building's leadership. For example, your related service personnel, mental health professionals, instructional coaches, resource teachers, etc. are all individuals who can add valuable contributions to your TLA. Imagine, if you will, the power of an interdisciplinary team of classroom teachers and mental health professionals, working together to revamp the social and emotional learning curriculum at a school. That would be powerful!

My personal philosophy about TLA work is to lean toward inclusivity and not exclude anyone who really wants to contribute. My main criterion for TLA candidates is their strong desire to participate. I like to help the teachers "self-select" themselves into the work. A good way to do this is to provide a solid understanding of the TLA, so they know what to expect and to what they are committing. Steps to recruiting candidates for your TLA are next.

## How Can We Recruit Teacher Leaders?

To recruit is to sell. If you build a meaningful and intriguing program *and* communicate your vision effectively, teachers will want to join this exciting opportunity. There is no singular blueprint to disseminate information to teachers about your TLA, but communication channels could include emails, memos, flyers, video presentations, in-person pitches, blimps, etc. I might recommend selecting at least two to three methods and leverage message repetition. It is helpful to provide a brief summary (Brevity is helpful to ensure that your words will be read, and the details can be added later.), which includes an invitation to an informational session. Though the specific media of messaging are your decision, the content of the messages throughout recruitment are very important to the eventual success of your efforts. Figure 4.4 displays a set of key messages to consider when recruiting teachers for a TLA. These messages would be ideally shared via an informational session in real time or through an informational video. Recall many of these messages from earlier in this chapter.

| | |
|---|---|
| **Why teacher leadership at our school?** | • Leadership needs exceed administrator capacities (distributed leadership).<br>• Teachers have valuable contributions to add.<br>• Highly effective schools display teacher leadership.<br>• We want to be greater than the sum of our individual contributions.<br>• Many excellent ideas have not been enacted because there has not previously been a forum to allow for their development. |
| **Why teacher leadership for me?** | • resume builder<br>• confidence builder<br>• skill builder<br>• empowerment<br>• can build/strengthen relationships with administrators and colleagues<br>• The students need our collective effort.<br>• I have something to contribute! |
| **Who should join our teacher leadership academy?** | • educators who answered "yes" to the questions in Figure 4.2<br>• educators who *want to be able to* answer "yes" to the questions in Figure 4.2<br>• motivated educators<br>• educators with growth mindsets<br>• educators who are interested enough to read this flyer/watch this video/attend this informational session (AKA *Me!*) |
| **What is our vision of a teacher leadership academy, and what would my commitment be?** | • number of sessions each year (5 has worked very well for us in non-pandemic school years.)<br>• length of sessions (i.e. half day, 2 hour, 1 hour, etc.)<br>• attendance requirements (compulsory vs. choice)<br>• topics for professional learning (proposed and to include a means for participants to share their preferences, perhaps through a survey) |

*Figure 4.4* Recruitment messages for a teacher leadership academy.

Of course, your creativity and latent talents might help to sweeten the deal and generate more interest, while still communicating these general messages. In the past, I have created simplistic animated videos, recorded screencasts, developed flyers, and met with individual teachers who were interested but could not make the informational session dates, among other methods. You should use the tools and talents you and your team have, whether they include humor, music, performance art, etc. The end goal is to generate excitement within members of your staff that this platform will be the valuable investment you know it will be.

Once you have generated interest in the TLA, and perhaps even held an informational session or sent a video to potential participants to share key information, it is helpful to formalize the onboarding of teachers into the TLA through an application process. This can be as formal as your team wants it to be. For example, if operating your TLA at a district level, you could require recommendations from teachers' building administrators and essays of intent from the prospective teacher leaders as part of a formal application. If within a small district or one school, you could create a simple application that resembles a short survey. Potential elements for a TLA application, including sample items, as well as their rationale, can be found in Figure 4.5. Note that recommendations from formal leaders would likely not be necessary if your TLA is operating at only one school.

From your applications, your team can make decisions about admission. As stated above, a group of about 5–20 participants is generally a practical size for dynamic sharing. Ultimately, you need to construct your desired group, based upon your facilitation capacity. For example, will a school principal be the sole facilitator of the group? Will a team lead this group? Or, will there be collaboration between district and university staff to facilitate the TLA, as is the case in my own TLA work in districts? Regardless of your answers to these questions, getting your interested teachers into the TLA is only the beginning. We next consider what to do with the group once you have them assembled.

## Teacher Leadership Academy: *How?* and *What?*

One of the first logistical questions to answer is about scheduling. If you have the luxury of available substitutes to cover for teacher professional learning,

# Building a Teacher Leadership System

| Element | Sample Potential Items | Rationale |
|---|---|---|
| work experience information | • Please state your first and last name.<br>• Share your school and your role there (i.e. Grade 3 teacher at RBG Elementary).<br>• How many years have you taught? | • know your audience<br>• track the range of the group (i.e. level, roles, experience, etc.) to eventually arrive at a diverse group |
| contact information | • Please share your email address. | • allows for contact with accepted members<br>• allows for the creation of a TLA email distribution list |
| professional learning interests | • From the following list of possible professional learning topics, please select all that interest you. (See later in this chapter about possible TLA content.)<br>• If an area for professional learning that interests you was not on our list, please share it here. | • know your audience (again)<br>• provide for informed professional learning planning<br>• later, strategic grouping of participants for projects or discussions |
| statement of interest | • Why do you want to participate in this TLA?<br>• What do you hope to gain through your participation in this TLA? | • know your audience (yet again)<br>• determine commitment level<br>• allow for differentiation among candidates, should it need to be a competitive process |
| recommendation from formal leaders | • Please include a letter of recommendation from your principal or department leader regarding your participation in this TLA.<br>• Please have your principal complete this recommendation form. (not included here) | • know your audience (but you already knew that!)<br>• identify possible challenges to participation<br>• in most cases, affirm to the teacher leaders that their participation will be supported by their leaders |

*Figure 4.5* Potential elements in a teacher leadership academy (TLA) application.

allowing teacher leaders to focus on their work during the school day, perhaps a half-day format can be favorable for a few reasons. First, teachers will appreciate that this work is being given priority, since it can take place during the workday. Second, teachers will not have to commit, at least for your formal meetings, to time outside their busy working schedules. Third, for teachers with after-school obligations, such as coaching or activity supervision, this model permits their inclusion. However, this model does not always work and, in some cases, is not preferred by teachers, who would rather not be away from their students and need to write substitute plans.

Another structure includes situating your meetings during previously established professional learning time. Though this idea can check many advantage boxes, it often does not work because you will be removing this small subset of teachers from, presumably, needed professional learning within their department or school. Another idea is to facilitate formal sessions outside of school hours. As implied above, this concept will sometimes exclude those teachers with other obligations, which is unfortunate. Given the various pros and cons of each approach, it can be helpful to ask the group for their preferences and/or restrictions, which can allow for maximal participation and minimal hard feelings. For example, by including an application question about availability, with a few possible choices, you can gauge what will work for your TLA.

Another factor to consider is how many sessions to plan and whether these sessions are compulsory or optional. From my experience, five sessions throughout the year, each ranging in time from two hours to half days (about three to four hours), seem to be a manageable number that can be spaced out to allow time for processing of information and, when applicable, work on teacher leadership projects. These sessions could be roughly spaced every other month, or at the initial phases when you are frontloading professional learning, monthly. The first two sessions with a new TLA could be devoted to team building and professional learning, while the third through fifth sessions could include some professional learning, with most of the time devoted to project work.

From a professional learning standpoint, your team would need to determine the topics and experiences that best meet your district and/or school needs. Further, as mentioned above, asking your TLA participants what topics interest them is a highly democratic and constructivist approach. However, there are some general topics that might have universal appeal to most TLAs. Some of these are presented in Figure 4.6.

# Building a Teacher Leadership System

| | |
|---|---|
| demystifying teacher leadership | team building activities |
| setting a TLA common vision | adult learning principles/facilitating professional learning |
| equity/social justice | leadership for change |
| difficult conversations | student engagement |
| social and emotional learning | teacher and educational leadership standards |

*Figure 4.6* Potential teacher leadership academy professional learning foci.

The open-ended, limitless nature of what to do with a motivated group of teacher leaders is a daunting consideration. However, the professional learning selected and pursued by this group can be a means to plant seeds about potential leadership projects, which are our next focus.

## Selecting Teacher Leadership Projects

The first question that arises when discussing leadership projects with teachers is: *Who determines what projects teachers undertake?* This is a complicated question to answer. In brief, teacher leaders should undertake projects that meet these two criteria: (a) the teachers are interested and motivated to pursue them and (b) formal leaders and leadership teams view these projects as valuable and aligned to school needs.

The former need should be obvious to readers. Namely, a TLA should be an empowering and exciting experience for teachers. As such, they should not be tasked with doing someone else's work or completing administrative tasks. That would be drudgery and a self-defeating way to operate a TLA! After all, as I asserted earlier in this chapter, agency for teacher leaders is a powerful construct. Choice in projects is a step toward building such perceptions of agency.

The second requirement is equally important. You will recall that I shared results from my own research with participants in TLA work, and it was apparent that administrative support was critical to project success. Thus, it is important to have formal leaders' endorsement of projects from the onset, which can avoid feelings of frustration and wasted teacher leader time later. I recommend that teacher leaders and formal leaders have a chance to interface directly about proposed projects. If there can be a formal meeting, excellent. If there can be a formal proposal for the leadership

# Building a Teacher Leadership System

| Teacher Leadership Academy Project Proposal |||||
|---|---|---|---|---|
| Project Title: |||||
| Justification: |||||
| Theory of Action: |||||
| Alignment to District Initiatives: |||||
| Connections to Leadership Content: |||||
| Statement of Impact to Students: |||||
| Project Proposed Action Plan |||||
| Action Step | Timeline | Roles Involved | Resources Needed ||
|  |  |  |  ||

*Figure 4.7* Teacher leadership academy project proposal template.

project, even better! Figure 4.7 displays the components of a TLA project proposal template to help teacher leaders comprehensively consider what they want to do. (Read: *They need to think through their idea in a concrete manner, so they are not too logistically lofty or naïvely simplistic!*) Teacher leaders present these proposals to their formal leaders. This format was adapted from my collaborative work in the Cromwell (CT) Public Schools (CPS), with the CPS Director of Curriculum and Instruction, Dr. Keri MacLean. We found this format helped teacher leaders better conceptualize their great ideas and segment them into logical "chunks" when pitching their proposals to others. An editable version of this template can be found in the eResources collection for this book.

Teacher leaders should be encouraged to propose projects that will have a wider impact on students, when possible. An isolated project to impact three students, while well-meaning, might not fully justify all the time and effort that will be invested. Further, the teacher leaders should be able to articulate a specific need that their project will address, so that they are not guilty of adding more to the school's full plate without good reason. The theory of action, without getting too technical, is generally written as an "If … then" hypothesis statement, followed by an explanation. If we do *this*, then the impact will be *that*, because …

Teacher leaders' projects should connect to larger organizational purposes. By requiring teachers to articulate these connections, like the need for justification, we ensure that teacher leaders' work will help move us where we want to go, collectively. We ask our participants to connect back to leadership content and standards we have discussed in our professional learning sessions leading to project selection, so they can truly apply their new skills. The connection to students should be self-explanatory, as any TLA project worthy of time and effort should impact students in meaningful ways (i.e. academic achievement, social and emotional outcomes, engagement, behavioral impacts, connection to school, access to opportunities, etc.).

The proposed action plans, which are somewhat analogous to the school improvement action plans shared in Chapter 2, provide teacher leaders the opportunity to fully process the logistics of their proposal. They should be answering questions such as: *Who will need to be enlisted to help? How will I convince my fellow teachers that this initiative is worthy of our time? How long will this step take? What will the steps in this rollout include? What might I do differently, if my first planned steps are unsuccessful? Are there any costs involved, and, if so, how might I obtain the needed funding? What professional learning will be needed to advance this initiative, and how can I facilitate this learning? What permissions will I need to obtain and from whom?* Teacher leaders who better answer these systems thinking questions are better positioned for success with their projects. Once teachers complete their proposals, it is helpful to coordinate an audience with their appropriate formal leaders to allow teachers to present their proposals, which can easily be translated into a simple slideshow presentation, if desired. This system will help to forge strong, informed support from formal leaders for teacher leaders' efforts.

I think I can anticipate your next question: *What do teacher leaders select as their projects?* I do not want to stifle anyone's creativity, so I often hesitate to provide too many specifics about projects. However, for those looking to build a TLA from scratch, concrete examples can be helpful to conceptualize the work. Again, projects are generally bounded by (a) teacher leaders' creativity and passion and (b) the support and endorsement from their formal leaders, which are often influenced, in turn, by formal leaders' beliefs about the appropriate nature and scope of proposed projects. Naturally, teacher leaders' ability to "sell" their proposal to their formal leaders is an important leadership lesson, by itself. Figure 4.8 offers some potential TLA projects to help your team begin thinking and dreaming. Do not let this list restrict your own ideas, but know that these have "been done" before.

It should be obvious, but I would like to note that teacher leaders can work independently or as a member of a team of teacher leaders. Collaborative work is always one of the powerful and desirable features

Building a Teacher Leadership System

| | |
|---|---|
| improvement of a process or system | teacher mentoring program creation/revision |
| instructional technology support/professional learning | creation of student programs: (i.e. SEL, kindness, citizenship, etc.) |
| equity leadership to improve experiences for traditionally marginalized groups | implementation of a peer observation structure, like collegial visits |
| wellness/social and emotional learning opportunities for adults | professional learning series/book club/lesson study |
| student-led conferences | mastery-based learning |

*Figure 4.8* Possible teacher leadership academy projects.

for participating teachers, so I encourage teachers to work together, when ideas and enthusiasm overlap. At times, teachers will join the TLA in pairs or groups, specifically so they can work on a particular project of mutual interest. Any configurations of leadership teaming are acceptable, though I caution you to discourage teams that get bigger than about four teacher leaders, since group dynamics can stifle progress and reduce their nimbleness. Once teacher leaders have selected their projects, provide the TLA members time to work at each subsequent formal meeting. Also, offer them a chance each session to dialogue with members working on different projects, so they can maximize their learning across teams. Having each team report to the TLA about progress and share problems of practice they are experiencing can help to spark this cross-group learning.

## Celebrating Teacher Leaders' Work

Creating and operating a TLA is an exciting venture, and teacher leader participants will have committed to extra effort on behalf of the children of your school and district. Thus, it is most appropriate that their work is celebrated and their time and commitment are met with appreciation and gratitude. Naturally, there are multiple ways for formal leaders to celebrate the accomplishments of teacher leaders.

First, it is a classy and respectful touch to present teacher successes in a public forum at the end of the school year, which could be a faculty meeting at a school level and/or a Board of Education meeting at the district level. Also, local newspapers and, certainly, internal district and school publications frequently share success stories. Your teacher leaders' accomplishments can provide excellent material for such positive stories.

It goes without saying that these types of public acknowledgment can provide teacher leaders with great reinforcement for their efforts, which is consistent with research about how effective educational leaders affirm their teachers' work (Marzano et al., 2005). However, there are other purposes for such public recognition. First, it is in the interest of all students to spread messages about successful practices, and other teachers can be equal parts illuminated and inspired when they learn about their colleagues' ideas. Second, the greater community (such is the case when teacher leaders are celebrated at Board of Education meetings) should know about the extra effort of teacher leaders to make the district and/or school a better place. This creates good will and support for school efforts in the community. I have always felt that many schools miss opportunities to build collective relationship equity within their communities, and celebrating teacher leaders' efforts and projects is one such opportunity not to be missed.

## Summary

Teacher leadership is needed because school leadership work surpasses formal leaders' capabilities. Further, the most effective schools display teacher leadership, which has, in turn, been shown to positively affect student achievement. Literature and teacher leadership standards vary in their depictions of teacher leadership work. These educators' responsibilities could include mentoring colleagues; sharing instructional resources; making decisions at a department, grade, or school-wide level; serving on committees or teams; organizing school events; as well as many more roles. Teacher leaders can have formal titles or simply be motivated to work within areas of interest and need outside their own classrooms.

A concrete way to empower teacher leadership in your school or district is a teacher leadership academy. This structure can be a vehicle to provide a motivated group of educators the opportunity to undertake professional learning together and then apply their skills through the facilitation of leadership projects in their own schools or across the district.

Only your school can determine the membership of a TLA. However, I recommend that you include those educators—not limited to just teachers—who are motivated to make a difference and want to participate. A TLA of

5–20 participants is generally a manageable group. Professional learning for the group can include school/district priorities and areas of interest from participants. Teacher leaders can select projects, either individually or in groups, in consultation with their formal leaders, and a project proposal can assist teacher leaders in conceptualizing and presenting their project vision. Teacher leadership work should be celebrated, both within and outside the school.

> **Questions to Consider for Chapter 4:**
> *Building a Teacher Leadership System*
>
> 1. What evidence of teacher leadership exists now in your school? What aspects of teacher leadership possibility would you like to see grow?
> 2. How could explicitly growing teacher leadership in your school impact the three foundational principles of *empowerment*, *collegiality*, and *risk taking*?
> 3. What is the capacity of your school and/or district to operate a teacher leadership academy? If there are roadblocks, what are these, and how can they be overcome?
> 4. In what ways could you recruit for teacher leadership academy participants?
> 5. In what ways, other than through a teacher leadership academy, can you support and nurture teacher leadership in your school?
> 6. What is a tangible next step for your leadership team after reading this chapter?

# References

Berg, J. H., & Zoellick, B. (2019). Teacher leadership: Toward a new conceptual framework. *Journal of Professional Capital and Community*, 4(1), 2–14. https://doi.org/10.1108/JPCC-06-2018-0017

Center for Strengthening the Teaching Profession. (2009). *Teacher leader self-assessment*. Author. http://cstp-wa.org/cstp2013/wp-content/uploads/2013/11/CSTP_self_assessment.pdf

Crowther, F., Ferguson, M., & Hann, L. (2009). *Developing teacher leaders: How teacher leadership enhances school success* (2nd ed.). Corwin Press.

Danielson, C. (2007). The many faces of leadership. *Educational Leadership, 65*(1), 14–19.

Diamond, J. B., & Spillane, J. P. (2016). School leadership and management from a distributed perspective: A 2016 retrospective and prospective. *Management in Education, 30*(4), 147–154. https://doi.org/10.1177/0892020616665938

Hairon, S., & Goh, J. W. (2015). Pursuing the elusive construct of distributed leadership: Is the search over? *Educational Management Administration & Leadership, 43*(5), 693–718. https://doi.org/10.1177/1741143214535745

Harris, A., & Jones, M. (2019). Teacher leadership and educational change. *School Leadership and Management, 39*(2), 123–126. https://doi.org/10.1080/13632434.2019.1574964

Johnson, S. M. (2019). *Where teachers thrive.* Harvard Education Press.

Katzenmeyer, M., & Moller, G. (2009). *Awaking the sleeping giant: Helping teachers develop as leaders* (3rd ed.). Corwin Press.

Leithwood, K., Louis, K. S., Anderson, S., & Wahlstrom, K. (2004). *Executive summary: How leadership influences student learning.* https://conservancy.umn.edu/bitstream/handle/11299/2102/CAREI ExecutiveSummary_How Leadership Influences.pdf?sequence=1&isAllowed=y

Leithwood, K. A., Mascall, B., Strauss, T., Sacks, R., Memon, N., & Yashkina, A. (2007). Distributing leadership to make schools smarter: Taking the ego out of the system. *Leadership and Policy in Schools, 6*(1), 37–67. https://doi.org/10.1080/15700760601091267

Marzano, R. J., Waters, T., & McNulty, B. A. (2005). *School leadership that works: From research to results.* ASCD.

Nerlino, E. (2020). A theoretical grounding of teacher leadership. *Journal of Professional Capital and Community, 5*(2), 117–128. https://doi.org/10.1108/JPCC-12-2019-0034

Nguyen, D., Harris, A., & Ng, D. (2020). A review of the empirical research on teacher leadership (2003–2017): Evidence, patterns and implications. *Journal of Educational Administration, 58*(1), 60–80. https://doi.org/10.1108/JEA-02-2018-0023

Ovington, J. A., Diamantes, T., & Roby, D. A. (2002). Early distance learning success story: The teacher leader program. *College Student Journal, 36*(3), 387–398.

Ross, D., Adams, A., Bondy, E., Dana, N., Dodman, S., & Swain, C. (2011). Preparing teacher leaders: Perceptions of the impact of a cohort-based, job embedded, blended teacher leadership program. *Teaching and Teacher Education, 27*(8), 1213–1222. https://doi.org/10.1016/J.TATE.2011.06.005

Shen, J., Wu, H., Reeves, P., Zheng, Y., Ryan, L., & Anderson, D. (2020). The association between teacher leadership and student achievement: A meta-analysis. *Educational Research Review, 31*, 1–19. https://doi.org/10.1016/j.edurev.2020.100357

Sinha, S., & Hanuscin, D. L. (2017). Development of teacher leadership identity: A multiple case study. *Teaching and Teacher Education, 63*, 356–371. https://doi.org/10.1016/j.tate.2017.01.004

Spillane, J. P. (2006). *Distributed leadership.* Jossey-Bass.

Spillane, J. P., Halverson, R., & Diamond, J. B. (2001). Investigating school leadership practice: A distributed perspective. *Educational Researcher, 30*(3), 23–28. http://www.jstor.org/stable/3594470

Taylor, M., Goeke, J., Klein, E., Onore, C., & Geist, K. (2011). Changing leadership: Teachers lead the way for schools that learn. *Teaching and Teacher Education, 27*(5), 920–929. https://doi.org/10.1016/J.TATE.2011.03.003

Teacher Leadership Exploratory Consortium. (2012). *Teacher leader model standards.* Author. https://www.nnstoy.org/teacher-leader-model-standards/

Torres, D. G. (2018). Distributed leadership, professional collaboration, and teachers' job satisfaction in U.S. schools. *Teaching and Teacher Education, 79*, 111–123. https://doi.org/10.1016/j.tate.2018.12.001

Visone, J. (2020). Empowering teachers through a PDS Teacher Leadership Academy. *PDS Partners: Bridging Research to Practice, 15*(1), 13–15. https://doi.org/10.36099/15.1.14

Visone, J. D. (2018). Empowerment through a teacher leadership academy. *Journal of Research in Innovative Teaching & Learning, 11*(2), 192–206. https://doi.org/10.1108/jrit-08-2018-0019

Visone, J. D. (2020). Teacher leadership for excellence in US National Blue Ribbon Schools. *International Journal of Leadership in Education*, 1–23. https://doi.org/10.1080/13603124.2020.1811897

Wenner, J. A., & Campbell, T. (2017). The theoretical and empirical basis of teacher leadership: A review of the literature. *Review of Educational Research, 87*(1), 134–171. https://doi.org/10.3102/0034654316653478

York-Barr, J., & Duke, K. (2004). What do we know about teacher leadership? Findings from two decades of scholarship. *Review of Educational Research, 74*(3), 255–316.

# Amplifying Teacher Leadership beyond the School's Walls

Juan and Karly, members of the English Department at Lincoln High School, were representing their colleagues at a conference of their state organization for teachers of English. Their department chair, Tiffani, had asked them to use the opportunity to bring new ideas back to their department. As they attended a workshop presented by a team of teachers and administrators from another high school about using the curriculum for civic engagement, the pair made some connections.

"This reminds me of the unit we created about social justice," Karly remarked. "They are choosing the informational texts and fiction selections, strategically, just like we did. Then they had the kids apply this information toward a project."

"I agree," replied Juan. "We use our curriculum to teach interdisciplinary content and engage students about their world, just like this project. It really is remarkably similar. I do like how they added a component about writing to local leaders. We could add something like that to our project."

"Good point. We should bring this up at our next department meeting. I am going to text Tiffani now. She won't believe what they are presenting."

Karly's hunch was correct. Tiffani, upon reading Karly's text about the civic engagement workshop, was also struck by the similarities between projects created by two separate teams in school districts many towns apart.

After the civic engagement workshop, the pair of English teachers joined a session about improving students' formal writing. This experience was offered by a pair of middle school teachers. Again, the two found the work to be familiar.

DOI: 10.4324/9781003190370-5

> "This reminds me of our writing boot camp that kicks off the year," stated Karly.
>
> "I was thinking the same thing," agreed Juan. "They have a similar structure, though they are coming at the issue from a lower level. We are teaching higher-level skills, but the basic set up is the same."
>
> "We could totally do this," Karly stated with confidence.
>
> "You mean this writing instruction model? We kinda already do something like this," replied Juan, confused.
>
> "No, I mean, we could totally *offer one of these workshops.*"

I agree with Karly and Juan, even though I don't know them that well. They could "totally" present at a conference. It seems they have some initiatives and curricular elements that would be worthy of sharing. The value of attending conferences and learning (i.e. through reading, coursework, or networking) outside of your school and district is that learners can both acquire new information and be reaffirmed in the value of their existing practices. Educators often notice how much they have in common with other schools and districts.

Educators, as attendees, can also see their own possible contributions. I have always found teachers to be a very humble and self-deprecating group, to a fault. Because the profession has not included a general culture of viewing each other's work regularly (a professional learning context for which I advocate vociferously in Chapter 3), teachers too frequently believe that others must surely be doing something better and more magical than what they are doing. Thus, they do not perceive they have something of value to contribute to their peers' learning. They do not see themselves as experts. Certainly, there are experts in our field, who have used the power of research to identify instructional strategies most likely to impact student learning (Dean et al., 2012; Hattie, 2009; Marzano, 2003; Marzano et al., 2001). However, this does not mean an individual teacher's effective pedagogical choices in her classroom context, especially in the rapidly dynamic environment of schools surrounding the COVID-19 pandemic, are not also valuable to share. The lack of confidence in sharing one's practice is a mindset—a rut, really—that leaders can help teachers escape. Leaders and leadership teams, through the consistent espousal and reinforcement of the three guiding principles, can provide teachers the confidence they need to share the great things they are doing with others. This is to the profession's

# Leadership beyond the School's Walls

benefit, overall, and the children of your and other schools will benefit from the sharing engendered.

Recall that the three guiding principles of this book are:

(a) **empowerment**: Our staff members feel competent and believe that they are equipped to make decisions in the best interest of our students and school. Our teachers have sound ideas that can improve what we do;

(b) **collegiality**: Our staff works together to solve problems of practice. We do not work in isolation. What we learn, we share; and,

(c) **risk taking**: We do not advance if we do not try new things and experiment. We are not afraid to do things differently.

Figure 5.1 also displays the three principles.

It is likely not much of a mental leap to envision how these three principles apply to teacher leaders sharing their learning and ideas with others. From an empowerment perspective, providing your teachers with the message that they have valuable ideas to share is a starting point toward building confidence. Collegiality is marked by sharing of ideas and practices. Finally, here, the risk taking is about teachers stepping out of the comfort zone of their own classrooms to become teachers to a group of unfamiliar adults. The first four chapters have focused primarily on the collegial sharing and leadership that teachers exert within their own building. This chapter will focus on teacher leaders sharing their ideas beyond their schools. We will start by examining why teacher leadership beyond the school is even important, and then we will consider teacher leadership at various venues and contexts beyond the school.

| | |
|---|---|
| **empowerment** | Our staff members feel competent and believe that they are equipped to make decisions in the best interest of our students and school. Our teachers have sound ideas that can improve what we do. |
| **collegiality** | Our staff works together to solve problems of practice. We do not work in isolation. What we learn, we share. |
| **risk taking** | We do not advance if we do not try new things and experiment. We are not afraid to do things differently. |

*Figure 5.1* The three foundational principles to empower teacher leadership.

## Why Consider Teacher Leadership beyond the School?

I know what some of you are thinking: *Jeremy, we are concerned with what we are doing with kids at our school. Why do we need to be concerned with what someone outside our school is doing?* This is a logical and reasonable question to ask. After all, the work of leading schools and educating children is complex and busy work. There is not a lot of "down" time that would be considered discretionary. We educators need to be judicious with our time. Thus, we should ponder the rationale for looking outside of our own schools' walls.

First, we need to return to thinking about schools as systems, as was discussed in Chapter 2. One consideration of systems thinking in education is the idea of an open system (Betts, 1992; Ribeiro, 2016). That is, schools operate within a context of outside influences, not the least of which are government mandates, local policies, and community and societal pressures (Shaked & Schechter, 2013, 2020). Thus, thinking of the work of educators as merely that which occurs within the four figurative walls of the school is incomplete, at best, and short sighted, at worst. Educational leaders should consider how their efforts to share what they do can impact those external influences on their schools. For example, if teachers, as a profession, can do better to explain what they do to their boards of education and policy makers, then those in positions to make decisions will be better informed to do so. Further, the better the profession learns from itself, the more likely that students, en masse, will succeed, and the public will view the educational system, on the whole, more favorably.

A second rationale for leading beyond one's school derives from our standards. National standards for practicing leaders and programs that prepare them call for educational leaders to look beyond their own schools to communicate about school and the profession's needs and advocate for support from the external influences on education (i.e. policies, funding, laws, etc.) (National Policy Board for Educational Administration, 2015, 2018). Further, standards for teacher leaders reserve intentional space for these leaders' work outside of their schools (Teacher Leadership Exploratory Consortium, 2012). These latter standards devote one of their seven domains entirely to teacher leadership work outside of their schools. In short, the standards suggest that a teacher leader "Represents and advocates for the profession in contexts outside of the classroom" (p. 47). Contexts include boards of education, legislative bodies, and other professional situations.

A third, and perhaps, most compelling rationale for aiming for teacher leadership outside of your school is the fact that highly effective schools display this attribute. In some of my research referenced in Chapter 4, I examined the practices of U.S. National Blue Ribbon Schools—those schools identified by their individual states as being exemplary at either (a) overall student achievement or (b) closing student achievement gaps. Specifically, I looked for evidence of teacher leadership activity. One of my important findings was the ubiquitous nature of teacher leadership in these schools. I also organized this activity into categories to determine what type of teacher leadership these schools exhibited. I found that teacher leaders in U.S. National Blue Ribbon Schools displayed leadership activity in these four broad areas: instructional leadership, school-wide decision making, driving change and professional learning, and leadership beyond the school (Visone, 2020). The latter category is the most relevant here. Teachers in these highly effective schools exhibited leadership outside of their schools, and you and your team should consider the increases in confidence, mutual sharing, broadened perspectives, and advocacy that can result from such efforts.

## Leadership and Sharing at the District Level

The first level of leadership beyond your school would be sharing across your school district. In some smaller, regional settings, this might mean stretching to other schools within your region that share similar characteristics. Let's consider how teachers can display leadership in this context. At a basic level, teachers can share resources with teachers in a horizontal or vertical way. For example, Grade 6 science teachers at one middle school in town could share lesson ideas and instructional materials with Grade 6 science colleagues at a different middle school. Teachers can also share vertically. Staying within the science department, your Grade 6 science teacher leader could share resources with teachers at the elementary level, high school, and other middle school grade levels. Thus, teachers can learn what expectations and experiences await students in each grade level. In addition to sharing within the educator ranks, consider sharing programmatic information with the district's Board of Education.

Leadership beyond the School's Walls

The Board of Education is a group of elected officials, many of whom are not educators, and it is a frequent practice in many school districts in the U.S. to have teachers and school leaders present aspects of their work to the Board for the purposes of edification and celebration. Many teachers are unfamiliar with what to expect at Board of Education meetings or how to present during them. To effectively present to your Board of Education, you first need to consider your audience. First, as a group of volunteers, who are often required to sacrifice time with their families to participate in meetings late into the evening, you will want to be judicious with your time. You might be given a specific time limit, and, if you are not aware of one, you should ask your district superintendent for a reasonable length for your presentation. If everyone presenting during a meeting drones on for 20 minutes (though everything you share will be super interesting and important!), the meeting might well extend into your next school day!

If you are participating as an invited guest on the agenda, you will want to create a focused presentation that captures the essence of your project/curricular topic/message. As short as this sounds, five minutes is likely appropriate. If you are creating a presentation, three to eight sparsely worded, picture-laden slides are reasonable. For presentations about classroom happenings, Board of Education members will want to learn how their budgetary and curricular decisions made a positive impact. Further, they usually like to hear from students, as well, so be sure to bring a few of them along! Figure 5.2 outlines features of a basic Board of Education presentation.

A solid presentation before your Board of Education can serve as a great advocacy centerpiece for your school. Since the standards call for formal and teacher leaders to assume an advocacy stance toward the profession, at large, and for their schools, these community interactions are opportunities

| free of educational jargon | approximately 3-8 slides (about 5 minutes) |
| includes student participation, when applicable | displays teacher leaders' passion for their work |
| essence of program/curricular topic/message is conveyed, without unnecessary detail | gratitude is expressed for Board regarding its support of your work and the students |

*Figure 5.2* Recommendations for Board of Education presentations by school leadership teams.

to build relationship equity (see Chapter 1) on a collective level. If you present your school and its work in a positive light, the Board of Education, and the tax-paying public that is monitoring the Board's actions and might be in the audience live or at home, might be more willing to support your school's work. In short, do not underestimate the power of your brief presentation to influence others' opinions of the value of public education.

## Advocacy and Sharing beyond the District Level

Related to sharing your successes and practices with your Board of Education, recall that standards for both formal and teacher leaders implore leaders from all roles to advocate for their school and the profession (National Policy Board for Educational Administration, 2015, 2018; Teacher Leadership Exploratory Consortium, 2012). Thus, it is important for leadership teams to use their influence and extensive knowledge of their schools to advocate for them in the community and to policy makers. Providing testimony at either the local, state, or national level, which will be addressed later in this chapter, would be one way to accomplish this type of advocacy on a wide scale and in a formal way. However, as the saying goes, "Charity starts at home." Thus, think of the many small moments educators have with parents and other community members. These informal opportunities can help these stakeholders better understand what your school needs from the community. They, in turn, can support your school through democratic processes. Uninformed voters make uninformed decisions. As educational leaders, we are obligated to help community members be informed, and, one could argue, that leadership through advocacy is just as important as the more typical instructional leadership. This is because advocacy can sway public opinion, which can lead to material support for schools and educators.

Advocating for the profession, at large, might take you into the local, statewide, or national political arenas. Policymakers at all three levels frequently need to hear from professionals in fields within which decisions are to be made. At the state level, laws are continually proposed that affect schools. Teacher leaders and formal leaders, with their in-depth knowledge of how schools work (or, at times, *don't*), are invaluable experts for the profession. There are seemingly infinite ways that educators can be advocates for the profession, at large, and we will consider a few such ways in the sections below.

In addition to advocacy, sharing your great ideas and practices, now that you have been empowered by the practices in the preceding chapters, can also take you beyond your own school and district. The profession benefits greatly from a broad sharing of practices and ideas. In this next section, we will consider a few methods to advocate for the profession and share ideas and practices, all at a larger scope than your own district. These methods include: testifying at public hearings, becoming active in educationally focused organizations (i.e. unions, professional associations, research organizations, etc.), presenting at conferences, writing for publication, and seeking grants.

## *Testifying at a Public Hearing*

Providing testimony about issues of importance to education is a valuable service to the profession. Those in positions to make decisions at the local, state, and national level are most often *not* educators. Therefore, your expertise and ability to teach others about the realities in the field are crucial to policymakers' accurate understandings of our profession. It is difficult to generalize this process, given the nearly infinite number of topics and settings where testimony from educational leaders could be valuable. However, there are some commonalities that can prepare you for such advocacy, taken from someone who has provided testimony in a variety of different settings and for varying purposes.

First, similar to a presentation to a Board of Education, know that there is likely a short time limit (Three minutes is a typical time allotment for public hearings at the state level.). Not only do you want to respect the time of your audience, but you must know that the presiding officers will likely ask you to "wrap it up," should you run over time. The legislative body will not let you continue to drone on, simply because you are a well-informed speaker. Second, it is helpful to make your position clear from the beginning of your testimony, so that the audience does not need to search your words for your purpose in testifying or wait to determine on which side of the figurative fence you sit. Third, make sure to identify clearly who you are, as a professional, and, thus, why you are qualified to provide the testimony. Fourth, in many cases, you will be allowed to submit written testimony along with your verbal, in-person testimony. I strongly recommend that you take advantage of this opportunity for two reasons: (a) written testimony serves as an unambiguous record of what you are sharing verbally, providing the audience of decision makers the opportunity to reference your written words that they might miss, both while you are speaking and after you are done speaking, and (b) written testimony is often not bound by limits, so you can give the abbreviated version of your thoughts via your spoken testimony, while the written testimony can expound upon these main points. Finally, your passion can be a great oratory tool, but too much emotion can reduce your credibility as a professional. It is better to be fact driven than emotion driven. Decision makers will be more likely to later rely on a quoted fact of a speaker, not the opinion of "that angry teacher," when deliberating on a vote. Figure 5.3 provides a generic template that can be used to craft a focused and succinct public testimony statement. Figure 5.4 provides a concrete, sample (and fictitious!) public testimony text, in case the template is too open-ended.

## *Educational Organizations*

There is no shortage of opportunities for involvement in educationally focused organizations. Your educator union, the professional association for a particular educator content focus area (i.e. mathematics, health and

---

Members of the <Name of Decision-Making Body>,

My name is <Your First and Last Name>, of <Your Town of Residency and/or Your School District> , and I am here today to speak in <Support of/ Opposition to Name of Bill, Law, or Policy>. Due to my work as an educator, I conclude that <Name of Bill, Law, or Policy> would have the following effect on students/educators . . . There are several reasons why I support/ oppose <Name of Bill, Law, or Policy>.

First, <Succinct Rationale with Evidence> . . .

Second, <Succinct Rationale with Evidence> . . .

Third, <Succinct Rationale with Evidence> . . .

In conclusion, I support/oppose <Name of Bill, Law, or Policy>. I appreciate the opportunity to speak before you. I also appreciate your time in listening to my testimony. Finally, I urge you to <Desired Decision-Maker Actions> because <Succinct Summary of Rationale Centered on What is Best for Students>. Thank you.

---

*Figure 5.3* Generic template for public testimony.

Leadership beyond the School's Walls

> Distinguished Legislators of the State Education Committee,
>
> My name is Ed U. Cater, of Happyville, and I am here today to speak in support of the proposed *Whole Child Supports Bill*. Due to my work as a public school teacher, I believe that the *Whole Child Supports Bill* would have a positive impact on students across our state. There are several reasons why I endorse the *Whole Child Supports Bill*.
>
> First, according to the Happyville Times, in a story last week, more than 16% of families in our state required food assistance in the last year. The socioeconomic needs of families find their way into our schools, via students, who are less likely to concentrate on their schoolwork, if they have food insecurity or they are troubled by financial struggles in their homes. The *Whole Child Supports Bill* would provide districts with needed resources to direct families to community assets that can support our families.
>
> Second, student mental health needs must be adequately addressed. According to the Centers for Disease Control and Prevention, up to 1 in 5 children in our nation experience a mental health challenge in a given year. This prevalence means that mental health services are not just for a few children. Rather, a significant segment of our school-aged population needs support. I see these needs in my own classroom. I have more than a handful of students who have difficulty coping with small setbacks. Other children are very anxious about our fast-paced curricula. Still others struggle to interact appropriately with their peers. The *Whole Child Supports Bill* will provide funding for school districts to hire more social workers, school psychologists, and behavioral technicians, and we need these experts to address student mental health challenges.
>
> Third, Social and Emotional Learning should become part of the regular school curriculum. It is as important as reading and mathematics. The Collaborative for Academic, Social, and Emotional Learning asserts that schools that prioritize Social and Emotional Learning house students who achieve more academically, treat each other better, and are happier and well-adjusted. The *Whole Child Supports Bill* would provide funding for this work in schools, while also legislating a uniform set of standards for Social and Emotional Learning.
>
> In conclusion, I wholeheartedly endorse the *Whole Child Supports Bill* due to its emphasis on meeting student and family financial needs, addressing student mental health challenges, and prioritizing Social and Emotional Learning. I appreciate the opportunity to speak before you. I also appreciate your time in listening to my testimony. Note that I have also submitted written testimony to accompany my words here. Finally, I urge you to vote to advance the *Whole Child Supports Bill* out of this committee because the students of our state need more from their schools than just academic outcomes. Thank you.

*Figure 5.4* Sample public testimony in support of a powerful, though fictitious, bill.

wellness, science, school counseling, administration, etc.), associations of Boards of Education, and education organizations focused on a specific aspect of the profession (i.e. professional learning, leadership, equity, etc.) are all potential forums for you to express your leadership. Most of these organizations have democratic protocols so that practicing educators can become part of the leadership structure. Attending meetings can become a great opportunity for networking and idea sharing. Of course, if these organizations are too large and seemingly too difficult to navigate, think locally and regionally, first. Many national organizations have statewide affiliates, for example. Participate to share what is occurring at your school, while seeking key insights from others that you can return to share with colleagues.

Consider the value of participating in a professional organization based upon important feedback I receive from teacher leaders with whom I have worked—that it is empowering and energizing to have opportunities to share ideas with other like-minded individuals. The credibility of all in the room suddenly increases when all participants have a common experience. If you are all science teachers, for example, you can all relate to the challenge of students supporting scientific claims with the available evidence. Shared experiences help teachers deeply examine issues, allowing participants to gain greater insight from conversations.

## Presenting Your Successes

Many educational organizations host conferences or other regular forums for sharing ideas. Nothing can affirm the collective confidence of a leadership team more than sharing members' ideas with those outside the school. It is easy to become locked into a rut or be lulled into thinking that every school has solved problems exactly as you have. To return to the challenge of humble educators unsure that what they do is worthy of sharing, which was discussed in Chapter 4, this challenge can apply to your entire leadership team. Your school—if you care enough about your processes and results that you are reading this text together—possesses practices that are worthy of sharing with others. Perhaps these successes are only occurring in pockets. So be it. Share those. No one will ever tell you at a conference that your school is not performing well enough to have something of value to share with others.

What are the benefits of sharing your work with others through presentations? First, the affirmation provided to you by those outside your school, who see value in what you are sharing, is a great collective confidence boost for your team, and this is empowering, in and of itself. Further, those presenting benefit from the collaboration that precedes such a presentation (Even solo presentations often require some legwork and collaboration behind the scenes.), and there is time spent to reflect upon what it is, exactly, that you do so well. There is value in being able to explain your practices in a manageable and understandable way for others. The process requires you to justify why you made the decisions you have. Inevitably, this process helps you to critically examine your own practice (i.e. *Why would anyone care about what we are doing? Why is this special?*), which, for most educators, results in improved practice.

In order to present, you need to first determine what is worthy of presenting, and you should answer this inquiry while simultaneously considering how this answer aligns with the aims of the organization to which you plan to present. Have an excellent language arts unit about the struggle for Civil Rights in the U.S.? Perhaps, a statewide association for teachers of English and language arts or a national, equity-focused leadership group might be an ideal forum. Once you have selected a proper topic and forum for presenting, you will likely need to submit a proposal to the organization. Most conferences have a specific call for presenters, wherein they provide detail about what your proposal should include and what presentations will entail. Figure 5.5 provides you with a list of frequently asked questions and answers for a conference or educational organization presentation.

Presenting your practice to others can be a very empowering experience, as you will, most often, receive affirmation for the great work you are doing and that your ideas have helped someone else think differently. Presenting as a team also has advantages. First, no one needs to bear all the presentation "burden." Further, you can collaborate with like-minded individuals, and you might view them in a different, more positive light, as they become a presenter to adults, rather than children. Finally, there is a team-building element in creating a presentation collaboratively and sharing with others what "we" do at "our" school. Consider what your school, department, grade level team, and/or leadership team have to offer other schools and how you might share this information. Construct an interdisciplinary presentation team of teacher leaders, administrators, other staff roles, etc., and you will align yourselves with the three guiding principles.

| Audience Considerations ||
|---|---|
| How does your chosen topic align with the focus of this organization? | These should align tightly! |
| Are you allowed/encouraged to interact with the audience, or is this to be a passive presentation? | Refer to the conference expectations. Talk to others who have been to the conference, or reach out to the organizers and ask. You do not want to plan for participation, when your presentation, only, is expected. If audience participation is allowed, oblige! |
| What does your audience know that you can take for granted? | Ex. Any educational organization already knows about constructivist learning, so there is no need to waste time on defining it, but do define less familiar terms. |
| Style Considerations ||
| How long should your presentation be? | It is tempting to "put everything in," but you will rarely have time for this. Make sure to leave time for questions. Defer to the expectations for the conference, and make sure to rehearse while timing yourself. |
| What type of presentation medium should you use? | The conference might specify, but the industry standard is to use PowerPoint, Google Slides, Prezi, etc. Be aware that something unique might not work on the computer where you are presenting, so it is typically wise to stick to the basics, if this is your first attempt. |
| How much content should you present on each slide? | Keep content on slides to a minimum and font sizes large to maximize audience attention and improve accessibility for those with visual impairments. |
| Content Considerations ||
| What are some key ideas you should convey? | Consider conveying: purpose, literature (in brief) that support your topic, what you have done, unique features of your work, what impact your efforts have had on student learning, next steps, answers to questions from the audience, etc. |
| How much is too much? | This is difficult to quantify, but it is unmistakable when you witness it. Don't be that presenter! Practice on your family and (*really close and honest*) friends. |
| How should you interact with the presentation medium? | Do not read the slides verbatim. I repeat, *do not read the slides verbatim*. Rather, use the points on the screen to remind you of what you want to say and then share these points. Speak directly to the audience, not the screen. |

*Figure 5.5* Considerations for educational presentations.

Formal leaders, empower your staff by demonstrating that their ideas are valuable, nurture collaboration via a formal sharing forum, and help them take a risk to expand their leadership influence by sharing ideas with others. Teacher leaders, raise everyone's level of efficacy by sharing your effective practices with others.

## *Writing for Publication*

Another method to forward the three guiding principles in your school is to encourage leadership teams to share their work via publication. However, if you are like most teachers and formal leaders working in preK–12 schools, you do not have extensive experience with sharing your ideas in this way. After all, there is so little time! Further, much of your writing energy is allocated to creating communications for students and families. Though not typical, sharing your expertise with others in the profession via publication can be an exciting process. There is an exhilaration with seeing your words in print, like I am experiencing as I write this chapter! Sharing your ideas with others in print is a means to "pay it forward" permanently. But how can educators navigate this unfamiliar territory?

First, it is important to know that there is a space for your ideas in educational publications. However, there are also many publications that are looking for something different than you have to offer. Unless you are doing research as part of graduate studies, or you just have way more free time than most teachers and formal school leaders, you are likely not conducting what is known as "empirical research." Thus, many educational research journals and publications are not the right venue for your practices. You will want to find one of many publications focused on practitioners like you. Publications such as *Educational Leadership*, *Kappa Delta Pi Record*, *Education Next*, *The Learning Professional*, to name a few, are (inter)national in scope, focused on education broadly, and they encourage submissions from practicing teachers and administrators, not just researchers. However, there are also periodical publications associated with many of the hundreds of state, regional, or national educational interest groups (i.e. unions, subject area associations, leadership associations, etc.) that are geared toward and crave content from practicing educators. I have no doubt that you have read or even regularly receive many such publications. If you have ever read an article, looked at the author's credentials, and thought to yourself, *Self,*

*I could write something like this!*, then there is no reason to hold yourself back. You could also consider the more contemporary blog universe and the more traditional local newspaper, which are even more open-ended and inclusive. In short, if you have something to share, individually or as a leadership team, you can find a forum and use writing as a tool to express your developing leadership beyond your school!

When sharing your ideas in writing, you must consider the publication's specific instructions. However, there are some general guidelines, as well. First, there are almost always word counts, and you must bound the discussion of your wonderful ideas within these parameters. I even had to rein in my own loquaciousness as I wrote this book! Relatedly, publications usually have information entitled "Write for Us!"; "Guidelines for Authors"; or "Submission Guidelines." These sections of a periodical or website will explain the focus of the publication, what they seek from authors, and how to present your ideas. If they want stories about classroom instruction, don't write about a parent engagement initiative. If they seek a practical application of theory, make sure to provide them both with the specifics of what you did, as well as the theory that has undergirded your work. In other words, give them what they want. The more your writing matches what they are seeking, the more likely your manuscript will be selected for publication. More considerations for publication are outlined in Figure 5.6.

In order to put forth your or your team's best effort in writing a manuscript for publication, consider these "dos" and "don'ts," taken from someone who has written for practitioner publications, newspapers, research journals, websites, and more. Do your homework about your target publication so that you match your content to its purpose. Do let others read your work and accept their feedback with open arms (as opposed to: *You just don't understand me!*). Do favor active voice and clear, direct writing. Do provide other educators, through your writing, ample details about the great initiatives and practices you and your team have implemented. Do write. By this I mean, recall the third guiding principle about risk taking. Writing for publication is a risk, given that you might not be rewarded for your investment of time. You might feel the sting of rejection. However, the potential reward is most empowering, while the journey to get there can, especially when you are working with a team, be collaborative and affirming of your work. Give it a try! You just might surprise yourself. You have something to share. Why keep it to yourselves?

| Audience Considerations ||
|---|---|
| How does your chosen topic align with the focus of this publication? | These should align tightly! |
| Are you writing to teachers, administrators, higher education professionals, the general public, etc.? | Refer to the publication's aim and scope. Read the publication to determine what is typically published and who the target audience is. |
| What background information does your audience possess? | Jargon usage, sometimes taken for granted in schools, should be minimized, unless you know that your audience has the same background you do. If you must use jargon, define these terms in text. |
| Style Considerations ||
| How long should your manuscript be? | Follow the word count provided by the publication. |
| What writing style issues should you consider? | In general, prefer active to passive voice (ex. "We applied student-centered principles." vs. "Student-centered principles were applied."). Leave contractions (i.e. they're, isn't, etc.) out when writing in a formal journal. In this book and/or less formal publications, they're fine (See what I did there?). |
| What about personal touches? | Read the publication to determine if humor and more personal touches have a place. |
| Are writing mechanics important? | Yes, in short. Your ability to communicate clearly and mostly mistake-free will definitely impact whether your work is selected, or not. If you are "grammar-" or "writing-challenged," (*You know who you are!*) make sure to have a colleague or critical friend read your work prior to submitting. |
| Content Considerations ||
| What is your purpose? | Are you trying to persuade? Are you trying to outline for another set of educators how you do something? Are you reviewing a helpful and thought-provoking book you read (*hint, hint* . . . )? Make sure you know your purpose and communicate it to your readers. |
| What are some key ideas you should convey? | This depends on your purpose, of course. If you are trying to persuade, make sure to include ample supporting rationale and reasons (*Read:* data) to make your point. If you are writing to share a program, make sure to give a solid rationale for undertaking it, followed by details that would allow another leadership team in another school to replicate your work. |

*Figure 5.6* Considerations for publication.

On the other side of the coin, here are a few "don'ts." Don't, in your excitement to get published, send your ideas to just any publication. Make sure to match your sharing of ideas with their desire to have them! Don't miss the chance to work with others, whether in the writing or revision stage. Your writing will always become stronger with others' input. Don't take rejection personally or get discouraged. I cannot emphasize this one enough. Everyone gets rejected for publication sometimes. Many educators are looking to publish their ideas. If a first publication does not want your work, move to another one. Further, expect that this process will be a lengthy one. It is not uncommon to have many months (or years, even!) between a manuscript submission and final acceptance. This is to be expected. Finally, don't talk yourself out of giving it a try, if you have the thought to write to share your ideas. Go for it! Be empowered, and let others benefit from your experiences.

## *Seeking Outside Funding*

Another concrete way to express leadership beyond your school is through grant writing. There are myriad sources for funding that exist at the local, state, national, and private philanthropic levels. There are also entire texts and courses devoted to this wide and open-ended topic. Here, I will provide you with some basic ideas to get you started. I do not need to provide a lengthy argument about why you should consider grant writing, as the primary motivation—*money*—is one that is easy enough to grasp. Also, as I mentioned above, there are many sources of grants available to educators in public schools. So, the money is there, but many educators are unsure of how to begin to look for it.

First, it is important to understand that grants typically come in two varieties: noncompetitive and competitive. Noncompetitive grants refer to those that are available to all who are eligible and apply. If you meet the funders' criteria, provide a viable application, and follow the funders' rules, you are generally funded. These grants are often large-scale, district- or statewide offerings. It would be atypical for a teacher-led team to acquire such a grant. Competitive grants refer to those where applicants are not guaranteed funding if they apply. In short, you are competing with other educators for these grants, and your task is to convince the grant funders that they should give their money to you, not the other teams. These grants are more likely to be the type awarded to teacher-led teams, so I will focus my attention here.

First, you might ask: *Where should we look?* Searching for grant money can seem daunting, at first, but there are a few places to start. The two largest public school teacher unions, the National Education Association (www.neafoundation.org/for-educators/) and the American Federation of Teachers (www.aft.org/funding-database) offer teachers the opportunity to explore grants that might match their ideas and needs. The United States Department of Education provides a searchable database for government grants (www.grants.gov/search-grants.html?agencies%3DED%7CDepartment%20of%20Education). The American Association of School Administrators, a national professional organization for school superintendents, provides a webpage with links to grant opportunities (www.aasa.org/content.aspx?id=1550). These are but a few of the many available starting places for educators seeking external funding sources for their school. It is important to work collaboratively with your building and district administrators, as districts may have policies surrounding accepting grant money.

Once you have selected a grant to which you wish to apply, the next task is to complete the application. Certainly, grant applications vary by grant purpose and funding sources. However, some commonalities apply. For example, analogous to presenting at a conference or writing for publication, educators writing grants need to closely match their proposals with the desired funding targets of the grantors. In other words, if the grant is focused on equity, your job as an applicant team is to clearly articulate an equity need at your school and propose a clear plan that will address that equity issue. Some considerations for grant applications can be found in Figure 5.7.

If the enormity of national and state grants is too intimidating, especially as you are just beginning to explore outside funding sources, consider that there are many smaller, local grant foundations, often associated with school districts, where small groups of educators can apply for smaller grants. For example, as a classroom teacher and building administrator, I recall being awarded small grants (less than a few thousand dollars) to purchase materials for STEM activities for students and to fund a visit to the school from a famous author of young adult fiction. These local foundation grants are excellent first steps into the world of external funding. Further, they require less paperwork for the application and accountability, after the awards are dispersed. However, the general important considerations, as outlined in Figure 5.7, remain the same. Work with your team to envision, propose, and, possibly, fund an exciting new project for your students! Money is available. Funding organizations are merely awaiting teams of educator leaders to earn it.

| Audience Considerations ||
|---|---|
| How does your chosen topic align with the focus of this grant? | These should align tightly! |
| To whom are you writing in the application? | You are writing to the decision makers for the grant. This is a persuasive piece, and your job is to convince them that your project proposal is more worthy of their money than the others in the pile. |
| Style Considerations ||
| What is the general writing style for a grant application? | In general, grant applications should be clear, factual, and persuasive. |
| What about personal touches? | A grant application is not the place for informality; however, you will want to bring your school to life. |
| Are writing mechanics important? | Yes, in short. Your ability to communicate clearly and mostly mistake-free will definitely impact whether your proposal is selected, or not. If you are "grammar-" or "writing-challenged," (*You know who you are!*) make sure to have a colleague or critical friend read your proposal first. |
| Content Considerations ||
| What is your purpose? | As stated above, your job in the application is to present a convincing argument that your proposal is, not only worthy of funding, but *more worthy* of funding than other applications the funders will read. |
| What are some key ideas you should convey? | First, provide demographic information about your school and/or community. Then outline the need for the grant money, usually via clear and convincing data. Then share what you plan to do with the money, including as specific of a budget as you can create. Finally, share how you will measure the impact of the grant funding, if you are not directly provided with impact measures by the funders. |

*Figure 5.7* Considerations for grant writing.

## Goal Setting for Future Leadership Efforts

In this book, you have learned about myriad systems-based strategies to empower teacher leadership, through the application of three guiding principles: *empowerment*, *collegiality*, and *risk taking*. As you complete your study of these systems and strategies, your leadership team can now consider

| |
|---|
| **Guiding Principle 1:** *Empowerment* |
| If our leadership team/we/I . . . <br><br> then our teachers will be *empowered* because . . . <br><br> as evidenced by . . . |
| **Guiding Principle 2:** *Collegiality* |
| If our leadership team/we/I . . . <br><br> then our teachers will display *collegiality* because . . . <br><br> as evidenced by . . . |
| **Guiding Principle 3:** *Risk Taking* |
| If our leadership team/we/I . . . <br><br> then our teachers will *take more reasonable risks* because . . . <br><br> as evidenced by . . . |

*Figure 5.8* Leadership goal-setting worksheet.

how you will move forward with the ideas with which you have interacted. What will you do first? Next? What will you hope to accomplish in a year's time? Three years? How do you plan to make your changes sustainable?

Figure 5.8 provides a goal-setting worksheet through which your team can commit to moving toward the ideals of the three guiding principles. An electronic and editable version of Figure 5.8 can be found in the eResources collection for this book. Note that this worksheet can be completed from the perspective of a leadership team or an individual. The worksheet uses a theory of action format to help your team connect specific leadership actions with logical outcomes and evidence of these outcomes. Kudos to you and your team for your commitment to improve what you do for the benefit of students, all through the empowerment of teacher leadership!

## Summary

Teacher leadership can and should extend beyond your school's four walls, as evidenced by the practices of highly effective schools. Standards

# Leadership beyond the School's Walls

for school leaders and teacher leaders also call for leadership beyond the school, and there are many ways to accomplish this. Teachers can advocate for their schools and profession and share their effective practices in formal and informal ways. Formal methods include providing public testimony, participating in educational organizations, presenting successes and practices at conferences and other professional convenings, writing for publication, and applying for grants. Considerations for all these methods of advocacy and sharing include audience characteristics, intended purposes and messages, amount of content to be shared, presentation style, and professionalism. It is empowering to lead beyond one's school, whether you are a teacher leader or formal leader.

As a leadership team, it is important to reflect on learning, always, and a study of this book's ideas is no exception. I provided a tool for teams to examine what they plan to accomplish with respect to each of the three guiding principles. This tool can translate your learning throughout this text into practical action steps.

## Questions to Consider for Chapter 5:
### Amplifying Teacher Leadership beyond the School's Walls

1. Consider how your team's leadership presently exists (or doesn't) beyond the walls of your school. In what ways have teacher leaders and formal leaders advocated for your school and the profession at large? In what ways have teacher leaders and formal leaders shared ideas and practices from your school? What were the forums for this advocacy and/or professional sharing?
2. What advocacy needs can you identify for your school? How can you accomplish this advocacy?
3. What compelling ideas or practices can your school leadership team (or individuals) share? What forums, venues, or publications match what you want to share?
4. For formal leaders: in what concrete ways can you support your teacher leaders in their efforts to advocate for and share beyond your school?

5. For teacher leaders: what specific ideas do you have about advocating for or sharing beyond your school? What do you need to accomplish what you have identified?
6. What are your reflections on your ability to empower others or be empowered through your study of this book?
7. How will you move the three guiding principles (*empowerment*, *collegiality*, and *risk taking*) forward in your school? With whom will you work to make this happen?
8. *What are you waiting for?* (This one is rhetorical …)

# References

Betts, F. (1992). How systems thinking applies to education. *Educational Leadership, 50*(3), 38–41.

Dean, C. B., Hubbell, E. R., Pitler, H., & Stone, B. (2012). *Classroom instruction that works: Research-based strategies for increasing student achievement* (2nd ed.). McREL.

Hattie, J. (2009). *Visible learning: A synthesis of over 800 meta-analyses relating to achievement*. Routledge.

Marzano, R. J. (2003). *What works in schools: Translating research into action*. Association for Supervision and Curriculum Development.

Marzano, R. J., Pickering, D. J., & Pollack, J. E. (2001). *Classroom instruction that works: Research-based strategies to increase student achievement*. McREL.

National Policy Board for Educational Administration. (2015). *Professional standards for educational leaders*. Reston, VA: Author. https://www.npbea.org/wp-content/uploads/2017/06/Professional-Standards-for-Educational-Leaders_2015.pdf

National Policy Board for Educational Administration. (2018). *National Educational Leadership Preparation (NELP) Program Recognition Standards—Building Level*. Reston, VA: Author. www.npbea.org

Ribeiro, J. (2016). Why school system leaders need to be systems thinkers. *Getting Smart*. https://www.gettingsmart.com/2016/03/school-system-leaders-need-systems-thinkers/#

Shaked, H., & Schechter, C. (2013). Seeing wholes: The concept of systems thinking and its implementation in school leadership. *International Review of Education, 59*(6), 771–791. https://doi.org/10.1007/s11159-013-9387-8

Shaked, H., & Schechter, C. (2020). Systems thinking leadership: New explorations for school improvement. *Management in Education, 34*(3), 107–114. https://doi.org/10.1177/0892020620907327

Teacher Leadership Exploratory Consortium. (2012). *Teacher leader model standards.* Author. https://www.nnstoy.org/teacher-leader-model-standards/

Visone, J. D. (2020). Teacher leadership for excellence in US National Blue Ribbon Schools. *International Journal of Leadership in Education*, 1–23. https://doi.org/10.1080/13603124.2020.1811897

# Glossary

**affirmation**  to notice, acknowledge, and appreciate the work of others

**collegial visit**  a professional learning structure through which teachers learn by viewing a colleague's instruction; distinguishing features include a predetermined focus for the visit, guiding questions, visiting team, and debriefing session that includes the host teacher

**collegiality**  condition where staff members work together to solve problems of practice; work is not in isolation; what staff members learn, they share; one of the three foundational principles in this book

**crisis team**  school team that responds to crises within the school, evaluates and adjusts crisis response protocols, and educates staff about their role in crisis situations

**data-driven decision making**  using information, usually from more than one source, to make informed decisions about instruction, student programming, and other school functions, such as engaging with parents and maintaining a positive school climate

**decisional capital**  teachers' ability to make sound decisions that are informed by their experiences and their learning from each other

**distributed leadership**  spreading the leadership workload and responsibility within an organization among many stakeholders in various roles and at different levels (i.e. formal leaders, teachers, support staff, etc.)

**district-wide data team**  representative team of stakeholders from across the district that analyzes district-level data to make informed decisions; receives information from and shares information with school-wide data teams

**empowerment**  condition where staff members feel competent and believe that they are equipped to make decisions in the best interest of their students and school; staff members believe they have sound ideas

# Glossary

that can improve what their schools do; one of the three foundational principles in this book

**equity team**  representative school team that discusses matters related to equity, provides leadership for staff discussions of systemic inequalities, advocates for equitable experiences for all students, and assists in recruiting a diverse staff

**five facets of trust framework**  vulnerability, benevolence, honesty, openness, and competence are identified as qualities of school leaders who engender trust among their staff

**human capital**  the learning and skillsets of individual teachers

**instructional data team**  group of educators with a common instructional focus (i.e. grade level, department, team) that analyzes data to make instructional decisions; receives information from and sends information to school-wide data team

**instructional leadership team**  representative school team that oversees professional learning; discusses curriculum, instruction, and assessment; and oversees school improvement academic action plan(s)

**leadership team**  representative school team that advises the formal leaders, solves problems, sets direction, and provides for participative decision making and distributed leadership

**norms**  a set of agreed-upon expectations and protocols for all members of a team, committee, or professional learning community that guide interactions and work within the group

**optimizer**  leadership quality that includes being a positive presence and voice, communicating consistently that the team can overcome obstacles and address challenges successfully

**(student) parent teacher organization**  engages parents in the work of the school and helps implement school improvement parent engagement action plan(s)

**professional capital**  combination of three other types of capital: human, decisional, and social

**professional learning community**  collaborative group of educators with a common focus, who learn together and use data to achieve common goals

**purpose statement**  concise outline of the stated connections of any team or committee to the larger organizational purposes (i.e. vision, mission, goals, etc.), as well as how this group will accomplish these purposes

**relationship equity**  the state of relationships with others, influenced by the quantity and quality of interactions between these individuals

# Glossary

**risk taking** condition where staff members are willing to try new ideas and experiment to see improved results; teachers are not afraid to do things differently; teachers are willing to speak up and share ideas; one of the three foundational principles in this book

**school climate team** representative school team that examines behavioral and attendance data and oversees school improvement climate action plan (i.e. positive behavioral interventions and supports, restorative practices, social and emotional learning, antibullying efforts, etc.)

**school improvement plan** document that includes areas prioritized for school improvement focus, key data examined to determine priorities, broad and SMART goals, and action plans with concrete strategies to achieve the stated goals

**school-wide data team** representative school team that examines school-level data, creates and monitors school improvement plan, communicates to staff about school improvement plan progress, directs work of instructional data teams (i.e. grade level or department teams), and shares information (in both directions) with both instructional data teams and district-wide data team

**security team** representative school team that creates and monitors school safety plan, monitors safety drills, and advises formal leaders about safety concerns

**SMART goals** any student, educator, or school-/district-wide goals that are strategic/specific, measurable, attainable, results-based, and timebound; are typically included in student progress reporting, teacher evaluation, and school (and district) improvement plans

**social and emotional learning** process through which all young people and adults acquire and apply the knowledge, skills, and attitudes to develop healthy identities, manage emotions and achieve personal and collective goals, feel and show empathy for others, establish and maintain supportive relationships, and make responsible and caring decisions

**social capital** the complete set of interactions among members of a group

**social learning theory** theory of human behavior that includes the role of observing and learning from others in acquiring new knowledge or skills

**student intervention team** school team that serves as part of the tiered intervention system; provides a forum to discuss student needs within academic, behavioral, and social/emotional areas and advises teachers and monitors progress

# Glossary

**system**   set of things that, when organized together, produce a pattern of behavior and accomplish something

**systems thinking**   to leverage knowledge about systems to problem solve and improve an organization's function through strategic decision making

**Teacher Leader Model Standards**   organized set of knowledge, skills, and competencies for teacher leaders developed by a group of many influential educational organizations known as the Teacher Leadership Exploratory Consortium

**teacher leadership**   condition where teachers' influence extends beyond their classroom duties; can include, but is not limited to, sharing teaching resources with colleagues, mentoring colleagues, participating in team/committee work, leading change efforts, assisting in school-wide decision making, facilitating professional learning, sharing school practices to audiences beyond the school, advocating for the school, etc.

**teacher leadership academy**   professional learning and empowerment structure through which active and aspiring teacher leaders can learn together and lead projects of interest to the teacher leaders and of value to their schools

**teacher self-efficacy**   the general belief of a teacher that she can affect student results

**team connections map**   visual display that outlines the relationships among different teams within a school

**TED Talk**   short, influential talks by experts provided online for free by the organization known as TED

**U.S. National Blue Ribbon Schools**   schools recognized each year by the United States Department of Education for either (a) outstanding performance relative to other schools in their state or (b) outstanding gap closing performance relative to other schools in their state

**zone of proximal development**   range of challenge that is ideal for new learning, where a learner is challenged beyond what she can presently do, but with enough support that the challenge does not overwhelm or frustrate